THE E FACTOR

THE E FACTOR

THE 21ST CENTURY GUIDE TO ENTREPRENEURIAL THINKING

PROFESSOR DAVID GIBSON, OBE

WILEY

Registered Office(s)

John Wiley & Sons, Inc., 111 River Street, Hoboken, NJ 07030, USA

John Wiley & Sons Ltd, The Atrium, Southern Gate, Chichester, West Sussex, PO19 8SQ, UK

Editorial Office

The Atrium, Southern Gate, Chichester, West Sussex, PO19 8SQ, UK

For details of our global editorial offices, customer services, and more information about Wiley products visit us at www.wiley.com.

Library of Congress Cataloging-in-Publication Data

Names: Gibson, David A., author.

Title: The E factor : the 21st century guide to entrepreneurial thinking / David Gibson.

Description: Hoboken, NJ : Wiley, 2023. | Includes index.

Identifiers: LCCN 2024021653 (print) | LCCN 2024021654 (ebook) | ISBN 9781394285488 (paperback) | ISBN 9781394285501 (adobe pdf) | ISBN 9781394285495 (epub)

Subjects: LCSH: Critical thinking. | Entrepreneurship—Psychological aspects.

Classification: LCC BF441 .G445 2023 (print) | LCC BF441 (ebook) | DDC 650.101/9—dc23/eng/20240603

LC record available at https://lccn.loc.gov/2024021653

LC ebook record available at https://lccn.loc.gov/2024021654

Cover Design: Wiley

Author Photo: Courtesy of the Author

Set in 13.5/16pt Bembo Std by Straive, Chennai, India

SKY10078950_070524

Contents

Preface

Welcome to *The E Factor: The 21st-Century Guide to Critical Thinking*. My new book focuses on helping people learn, develop and survive in the global economy.

I have been helping people and institutions acquire entrepreneurship and innovation skills over a twenty-year period. The new technological revolution has increased the need for everyone to develop these skills to deal with constant change and challenges.

This book will provide you with the E-Factor skills to succeed and will enable you to make an impact on your area of work and help others to do the same. It is important that you not only read the book but complete all related exercises and apply the strategies within your own area of expertise. You will acquire both the knowledge and the capability to achieve your career and business goals.

This is your opportunity to become part of a global community of practice. So, enjoy the book, practise daily and make a significant contribution to your organisation and your community.

Best wishes.

Professor David Gibson, OBE

2024

THE E FACTOR

THE FACTOR

Part I

The Eight E Factors

I decided to write this book in three parts.

The first part discusses the eight competencies related to the E Factor and how you need each skill to develop and grow in today's changing economy. The eight E Factors are:

1. Resilience
2. Finance
3. Creativity
4. Negotiation
5. Personal Branding
6. Strategic Thinking
7. Leadership
8. Personal Influence

Chapter 1

Resilience

If I had to encourage you to have one skill that would increase your chance of surviving and thriving in the global economy, it would be to develop resilience.

At times, the word is overused but I'll explain what it means and how you can develop it.

It is the capacity to anticipate setbacks and crises. That seems a little negative, I know, but the reality is that not everything will go according to plan. The Fourth Industrial Revolution and the technological impact will bring constant change and challenges.

As an entrepreneur and a lifetime adviser to other entrepreneurs, I have found that many people expect that everything will go to plan and will be straightforward. However, business and your career will provide both opportunities and setbacks – sometimes at the same time! Sadly, I have seen many people give up great ventures and careers when the inevitable first obstacle appears.

People tend to believe you are born confident or an entrepreneur and some people have lucky breaks, and some don't. During my time as an enterprise educator, I have heard many highly intelligent people tell me it's all down to luck as to how you and your career turn out.

Nonsense. Certainly, genetics and upbringing have an influence, but you can still have a significant impact if you are prepared to learn and find new innovative ways to meet challenges.

You can be resilient, learn from your mistakes and achieve your goals whatever happens, but you must be prepared to learn. It is not enough to have knowledge – you need to find the right strategies and change your own behaviour and mindset to survive and thrive in this colourful arena of change. You live in a different world, one that is more uncertain than the one your predecessors faced, but arguably with more opportunity as you can potentially have more global opportunities than the previous generation.

The questions are: Will you be prepared to learn the skills and the mindset? What are these? How can you learn them?

Without good resilience you might miss significant opportunities, but you will acquire the skillset. Knowing about the theories is not enough. Let's review these skills and develop a plan together so that this core skill/mindset will allow you to welcome both challenges and opportunities.

1. The first thing is to be self-aware, so ask yourself: Are you resilient? How do you act in a crisis? What do others think about your ability to cope under pressure and deal with unexpected challenges? Ask a variety of people so that you can measure the response, and look for brutal

honesty no matter how sensitive you are, and a range of responses to improve the validity of the feedback. This is something you should do on an ongoing basis.

You may not like some of the responses but if the feedback is from a variety of people these responses can provide valuable analysis on the areas you will have to work on. It is important to learn how to fail, without it destroying your dreams.

Sometimes you might feel it would be nice to avoid feedback that is indicating areas of weakness but responding to this in an appropriate and positive way will save you years of heartache and provide the opportunity to be even better prepared for future challenges.

2. What is your physical health like? The stronger and fitter you are, the better prepared you will be for any potential crisis or opportunity. What is your weight? How fit would you describe yourself?

At one point in my life, I was unfit. I was also working extremely hard, long days and hours, with poor sleep. Then I had a health scare which encouraged me to embrace physical exercise and examine my lifestyle. I now run 5 k every morning and eat healthier.

This enables me to cope much better with pressure and unexpected events. If you are physically fit, it helps with your sleeping and lifestyle.

I am not trying to turn you into a fitness fanatic but instead to make you aware that physical health plays a part in helping you manage your energy levels and be more productive in your work. You become better prepared to deal with unexpected events, crises and even those great opportunities. Develop a plan and realise that physical and mental health are vital tools for you to use.

Make a realistic plan, one with no pressure to do too much at once if you are trying to create good habits and behaviours that last. Whichever physical exercise you choose must be appropriate for your age and personal background. You also need to find something you enjoy as you are more likely to turn it into a habit. Is there a sport you like or a class to attend which is fun? The more enjoyable and convenient it is the more sustainable the impact.

Personally, I find t'ai chi to be an exercise technique that provides physical and mental health benefits and is appropriate for me. It can be practised in a group or on your own and you do not need any specialist equipment or venue.

Ultimately, you will only keep doing a physical fitness programme if it is simple and easy to undertake, with a dash of enjoyment. The key is little and often, and be aware that healthy food can enhance your physical and mental well-being.

Your mental health is equally important. There is pressure to constantly be productive, which can induce stress. This can then lead to anxiety, which is not good for either your physical or mental health. You might be young and fit at the minute, but stress can sneak up, and you need to be able to recognise when to switch off from work and learn how to relax your mind and body. Bringing yourself into a natural state of balance helps to make you more productive, more successful. What is the best way to do this?

Mindfulness is a word you will hear often, and it plays a significant role in improving mental health. It is the capacity to relax physically and mentally at any time, learning to focus your mind on what is going on now around you and how you are feeling, but remain detached so you do not respond or react. Learning strategies to help you relax and gather your physical and mental strength are important. Learning to breathe deeply and slowly can help to reduce any potential imminent stress. One amazingly simple exercise you can practise is to breathe through your diaphragm. Slow breath in for five and out for ten. It's the outbreath that helps you to remain calm. The most important thing is to be aware of how you are feeling, and what might need to change.

The key is learning to be mindful in the moment by not reacting immediately or giving into your emotions – taking a little bit of time to adjust and refocus will prove useful. It is all about controlling and reducing any anxiety, which unfortunately has become all too common in today's business world and particularly since the Covid-19 pandemic. There are a variety of techniques you could experiment with to find what works for you.

If we can learn to accept that life moves around us at distinct levels, sometimes high sometimes low, then we can become more resilient and respond in the appropriate way. The calmer and more relaxed you are in your response to different challenges the easier it will be to find solutions and the better you will feel physically and mentally.

This strengthens your resilience. Some people are naturally calm and relaxed in all situations – perhaps personality and life experiences have taught them to take their time and relax when a problem arises. The rest of us need simple strategies with good impact.

My wife is a professional relaxation therapist, therefore I benefit and learn techniques first hand. As a meditation teacher, she ensures we start every morning with a 10–15-minute meditation. It is a myth to think you must meditate for at least an hour, 10–15 minutes is beneficial. When you are relaxed and focused, you are much more resilient and much more likely to solve challenges and problems as they arise; therefore you become resilient.

I am not saying you must do meditation to be resilient but what you must do is understand your own stress levels and triggers, and how you cope with them. We have many more triggers now than ever before, with technology changing regularly, and our dependence on it, and how we use it. Many people find themselves in stressful situations at work and at home. This is why many people are reluctant and frightened to run their own business and find it difficult to separate home and work life on an even balance. It makes sense to find several simple strategies and techniques that will not only provide solutions but will enhance your well-being and improve your resilience significantly no matter what you face.

There are many apps around and authors who specialise in helping you to find the appropriate techniques that may suit you. You can learn and adapt more than one technique and use them in different scenarios, and all will increase your resilience.

Find what works best for you and have the strategies to remain calm whatever comes up. Not always easy I know, but when you find or create what keeps you calm your resilience level will be extraordinarily strong.

Resilience is your capacity to deal with the changes we all face in the 21st century. The more you look after yourself the less anxious you will be when challenges appear at any stage. You will bounce back whatever unexpected changes and challenges arise. You will also have the confidence that you are ready for anything. Learn to be calm in the eye of the storm. Clearly, how you respond to sudden change may be the key quality or skill we all need. No matter what our background or ability we all need to learn to bounce back in unexpected circumstances.

The Building Blocks of Resilience

One of the most sophisticated models that anyone can learn with proven effectiveness is the model of Martin Seligman of the University of Pennsylvania, the creator of positive psychology.

He created a highly effective research-based model for resilience building in the US army. His model is called 'PERMA', with a focus on Positive emotion, Engagement, Relationships, Meaning and Accomplishment. It is recommended you work on them one at a time.

Can you remain positive in what looks to be a negative and challenging situation? It's your choice, make the right one. People who are negative with you should be used as fuel for a positive response. Enjoy proving them wrong. If you have ever been written off before you will know it can be great motivation. I was once told by an eminent academic from Queens University, that my enterprise education programme would never work. It became the number one model in the world within two years. You always have a choice as to how you react to negativity or discouragement. You can always control your response.

Keep doing the work you love and engage with externals, who are not involved in your organisation. This will keep your motivation up. You will also need people inside and outside your business or organisation who believe in you and will support you completely. This gives you the determination and the belief to keep going in tough times.

A small but motivated team can produce outstanding results. Find the people who will be with you no matter what. You only need a few and be open minded. It can be the most unexpected people.

Keep focused on your strategic purpose and you will be unstoppable. Always be focused on where you want to be and know that opportunities will appear. Celebrating small achievements will keep you motivated. One time I was making little progress, but I still believed in what I was doing. I re-evaluated how I was spending my time and how I was applying the E Factor.

One small opportunity to work with some environmental students became my first victory, and that taste of success was enough to raise my spirits and give me the passion to soar.

The best time to create habits to motivate yourself are at the start of the day and the end of the day. I am incredibly lucky my wife without fail gets us to meditate and say mantras first thing in the morning. I can honestly say I feel amazing and powerful at the end of those 15 minutes. Set your intention each morning to have a successful day.

It is also good to finish your day with gratitude for any lessons learned and the victories gained. Keep a small journal to highlight the good things. Celebrate the wins no matter how small.

Can you be grateful for the opportunity to learn lessons when things are not going according to plan? This is when you apply your resilience skills.

Remaining calm is a daily challenge but it is one that will keep you going.

Keep your belief and enjoy the learning. Learn to go lightly and laugh each day. Believe that one day you will look back at this and realise that no matter how bleak it may have looked in the short term, you persevered and saw it through. Once you get a small opening, jump into action – take that leap of faith.

Like many people I find myself being positive to others facing negative challenges but extremely hard on myself. Go easy on yourself. We are alive, we are learning, and we will get there. You can be an unstoppable force. Just take time, get your plan, and action it.

Take time to visualise your day and rehearse your responses. There is no guarantee that everything will go according to plan, but you will increase your chances that it will happen. Visualisation is a powerful tool for you to have in your skills box, and always keep your visualisation positive.

The mind is a powerful force. Choose to reframe your thoughts and keep them positive. It isn't always easy but keep persisting. Those who are resilient and keep learning, keep putting positivity out there together with action are an unstoppable force. Are you up for it? Give up the rollercoaster rides and be empowered by what you can control.

There is unmistakable evidence now that resilience skills can be taught and need to be. I do understand that changes can challenge our anxiety and push up the stress levels but if we can accept this and work on positive responses as opposed to reactions there are massive opportunities to learn and grow.

So how can you prepare for this? Practise thinking positively under pressure. Focus on what you can contribute. Should you begin to feel overwhelmed, distract yourself and refocus, and breathe – slowly, deeply and gently.

Why do you need to keep learning? Well, you may have been trained in how to pass exams, could you train another person? We will all need to interact with new people and innovative ideas.

Put yourself into situations that will require you to use these E-Factor skills and then begin to teach someone else. That will really increase your learning.

The reality is that you must, as part of your resilience strategy, take control of your own learning.

As part of your resilience development, you must learn what is needed now. It's an exciting time to be learning and developing and part of your resilience training is to accept this and prepare yourself to prosper and succeed as a global citizen.

You will become more adaptable than the previous generation. Accept that you must learn differently and that much of your learning to date is of limited use in training to be a global citizen.

Perhaps one of the finest examples of adaptive learning I have seen recently has been the new wellness training designed by Hilary Scott, a professional relaxation therapist in Northern Ireland. Noting that people either attended a mindfulness class, a meditation session, t'ai chi, or yoga, for example, she created a programme that brings the six biggest stress relievers and relaxation techniques into a one-hour session – 'Six in Sixty'. The variety of learning and the impact on our mind and body is incredibly significant and inventive. Most of us lose attention after the initial impact of achieving the feel-good factor, and our mind begins to wander. Hitting that spot six times in an unusual way has an incredible impact on our mind and body. If you're going to be resilient in this new world, this is an example of a model that could benefit you.

Creating and Implementing Your Resilience Plan

There is a significant difference between creating a plan and turning it into a workable model.

It is noticeably clear that building resilience is vital in the global economy where changes occur swiftly, depending on events that happen in one country impacting on other countries around the world.

Resilience is the keystone to any change or development plan as the nature of the Fourth Industrial Revolution ensures that constant adaptability and innovation is required to keep projects on track.

Key staff and leaders need to have developed unconscious competency and the habits to ensure they cope with change on any scale, not only to safeguard the project but also to keep their own mental and physical states at a healthy level.

Any organisation and its employees need to be able to cope with change, adapt and perform in a variety of circumstances. Plans need to be put into place to make the team high-level resilient performers no matter what internal or external challenges the organisation faces.

Individual, team and corporate resilient plans must all interlock and be adaptable to the level of corporate change required. Without this in place not only are individuals and teams vulnerable but potentially also the organisation.

Opportunities and Threats

Occasions will arise for organisations and key individuals to take advantage of new opportunities, both on a personal and corporate level. However, if the response is not adequate there will be significant threats to the sustainability of the organisation at all levels. Due to technological shifts, there is a strong likelihood of uncertainty and of challenges and opportunities that any organisation must meet and where possible use for the benefit of their long-term competitive advantage.

Individuals and teams do not always respond well to change and want to preserve the status quo; this is not possible now. Organisations now understand that change and technology challenges are here, bringing stiff competition. To work effectively with others, they need to understand that where resilience has not been embedded into the skill set on a corporate or individual basis there will be a threat on some scale to corporate performance and staff competency.

The reality is that outside pressure will not allow organisations to ignore internal or external threats. Resilience must therefore be embedded not only at executive level but also throughout the organisation.

The stronger the habits and the links between teams the better chance the organisation has of long-term survival. Many situations present both opportunities and threats to corporate survival and progression. The organisational plan must take account of this. There are similarities in organisations, except in small businesses run by individuals. They depend very much on the individual resilience of the owner or leader while large organisations are much more complex.

Your responsibility as an individual is to be prepared to learn and adapt, seek help where appropriate and monitor your progress on an ongoing basis. Your commitment to life-long learning is key here and adaptability and innovation will be required. Understanding your organisation and the threats and opportunities it faces is paramount. Developing and implementing the right habits and behaviours is vital to survival and growth.

How Is Resilience Achieved?

Resilience should be adapted as the key corporate and individual habit with ongoing training and monitoring.

External audits of performance levels are important with the need for corrective action mandatory where appropriate.

Eventually all anyone can do is to build and maintain their own personal resilience and support others where possible to do the same.

Everyone is responsible for their own behaviour or habits and if you have responsibility for others, you must support and encourage them. As an individual, whatever your job or business, you must first focus on your own development. Ultimately you must be responsible for building your own set of skills.

If you are a senior manager or a business owner you may have to encourage others to do the same, but your main responsibility is to look after your own personal development and where appropriate encourage others.

There is no point focusing on resilience habits once a month, or once a week. It is much better to spend 15–30 minutes every day. You are also setting an example for other people you might influence. To obtain the correct mindset, you could begin your day with some meditation, mindfulness or relaxation practice not lasting longer than 15 minutes. End the day by writing up your journal for 5 minutes. Focus on the following. What did you learn? What are you thankful for today? What would you like to achieve tomorrow? What could you have done differently today?

Keep your practices short and simple to build up the habit and routine. You are trying to achieve a practice that you would miss if you didn't keep it up.

A habit every day is more likely to happen if you keep it short, simple and consistent – it is less likely to be affected by any outside events and more likely to become a daily regime and will be much more effective.

Master resilience and you are ready to use the other E-Factor competencies to achieve your dreams and help others.

The words of Rudyard Kipling, in his famous poem 'If', resonate with me: 'If you can keep your head when all about you are losing theirs and blaming it on you'. It will help you perform well, cope with pressure and use the other E-Factor competencies to achieve results.

Chapter 2

Finance

You need to understand finances and manage money appropriately.

It is a principal element, and you want to handle your finances well so you can achieve your goals. There is certainly more to life than totally being focused on achieving financial wealth at all costs but try doing without it and life will become significantly challenging.

Handled in the correct manner money will help you make a greater impact and ensure the survival of your projects and career.

The good news is that anyone can learn to handle finances to make projects happen and achieve their goals. You will not need to be a mathematician and you do not need to study to be an accountant either. I became a qualified accountant and spent years in the financial sector thinking this would help me to progress. It soon became clear that I should not have spent all that time when my passion has always been to help people develop their skills and mindset to achieve their dream.

However, funding always plays a significant part in establishing any new project and can enhance your life and opportunities. So, learn the basics. Understand financial jargon and make it work for you.

Make sure you are numerate and have a concise understanding of how money works for you and make money a force for good. You can ask someone for financial advice, but you need to have a level of competency yourself to check their advice and ask the right questions. Use it to your advantage and help others.

How?

Develop good financial habits and be aware that when you handle money correctly you are more likely to achieve your dreams and create a plan for your long-term retirement.

Having financial independence at any stage will give you better opportunities. Handle it wrong and your lack of money or financial understanding will hold you back. Money is a tool to be used to achieve your goals. Good financial habits can only enhance your career and development.

There was an interesting program recently on Boris Becker who became Wimbledon tennis champion at seventeen and became a multimillionaire at an incredibly youthful age.

Unfortunately, poor mishandling of that money and poor financial decisions led him to bankruptcy, the break-up of his relationships and two years in prison. It's not always how much money you have but how you handle it!

Too much money too young led to Boris behaving like an idiot and some silly decisions cost him a lot. So, take heed. The key lesson is that it is not always how much money you have but how you handle it! Build a good relationship with money and you can achieve your dreams and help others. What could be better? Develop habits that will enhance your life in general, your career and your long-term future. Money will always play a part, but it can be hard to manage.

Let us learn the basics with a set of ten rules.

1. What are your financial habits at the minute? The good, the bad and the dangerous. I am happy to review anyone's checklist but let's look at the fundamental rules for financial success and sustainability. Are you confident with financial jargon or do you find it all rather boring? You only need to be competent, so don't be put off by financial jargon. Always question everything and be cautious of anyone giving you financial advice.

2. Try to spend less than your income. There may not be much left over, but this is a good habit to develop. People wonder how Boris Becker or some other famous pop stars ran into financial difficulties. Quite simply, they spent more than they had, even if it was millions!

   Perhaps we could be a little more understanding – it can be hard to keep your head when you suddenly receive or earn a significantly higher income. There will also be a lot of people who want to help you spend it! This can be heady stuff, and I speak from experience.

3. Ensure your taxes are kept up to date.

4. It is recommended you save 10 per cent of your income not only for a rainy day but also to take advantage of bargains or for the unexpected.

5. Understand and accept that you need to be financially competent. Money will always play a part in your life. Look at a side hustle, as it's called – something that could

supplement your income. What do you like doing that could boost your earning potential? Build some assets that will enhance your financial worth eventually. This could be buying your own house or making some spare income from a hobby you have.

6. Work at understanding financial jargon so no one will be able to dupe or deceive you.

7. Keep an open mind around other sources of income, and look around for those opportunities.

8. Claim whatever grants or benefits are available for you.

9. Do not lend money or borrow any except for a significant long-term investment such as a house, or piece of land.

10. Develop a good money mindset. Knowing your ability to handle your finances gives you this – which is a strong cornerstone in your life.

Financial Habits

Your habits will dictate your future and expose your strengths and weaknesses. Starting your own business part time could be the answer. Ideally offer people something they want that you are skilled at and interested in. It is also amazing the amount of financial grants that people are eligible for, which they don't claim through lack of knowledge.

Some Areas You Need to Study

Debt and money management. You want to be in control of any debt you incur. Debt plays a big part in handling finances correctly. You will need to examine your spending habits closely, and maybe curtail them. We can easily be encouraged by others and then debt can spiral out of control – leaving us feeling overwhelmed and affecting other areas of our work. Keep control of any debt.

There are great opportunities out there for anyone who can find their niche, keep their head and learn their lessons. You can do it!

Keeping Track

It should be easier for all of you with all the apps available to keep track of money, but you also need to use your creativity to create new streams of income. People can have good and bad attitudes to money. Hopefully using all the E-Factor competencies will help you achieve your financial goals. Along the way you will learn some lessons, make some mistakes, which is all part of the journey. Just don't repeat the same mistakes, learn from them.

Let me show you briefly how to use the other seven E-Factor skills to achieve financial success.

1. *Resilience.* Keep learning about money and the challenges it brings. Take an interest in rates for saving and or borrowing. Shop around for the best deals. Can you take advantage of them?
2. *Be creative.* Use your imagination to create ideas and find your alternative income sources by thinking creatively.
3. *Be strategic.* Think ahead and set some long-term financial goals and make well-informed decisions.
4. *Personal branding.* Get your profile out there, use the apps and marketing tools available and make good connections online. Find your niche and potential customers.
5. *Negotiation.* Learn to haggle and barter. You don't always have pay the cover price – ask for discounts and look for good deals. There is no need ever to pay the premium

price for anything. It takes confidence, but the more you do it the easier it will become. Remember – 'everything is negotiable'.

6. *Teamwork.*Work with friends you can trust on running little part-time projects. Inspiring others helps you to motivate yourself. It is good for your health to work as part of a team. Highly connected teams are more successful.

7. *Personal influence.* Could you learn to sell yourself or your projects on a part-time basis?

Excellent communication skills, including listening and speaking and building rapport, can bring you financial opportunities. Keeping a clear head and never getting too excited about any financial opportunity will serve you well. Understanding the language of money is vital. Do not let the jargon mislead you or bore you. Refuse to be misled or confused by financial jargon. Be open to learning its language.

Financial Jargon

Banking and financial professionals and institutions seem to have a language of their own and this does not enhance our confidence in handling our own financial future.

It can be useful to have a good financial adviser for complicated issues, but it is more important not to be confused or misled deliberately by financial and banking language. Money and financial products have a language of their own. You cannot expect to become a financial expert overnight but money and your handling of it will play a significant part in you achieving short-term and long-term goals.

So, let's tackle some jargon to see if you are determined to understand the language clearly and become less likely to be misled or confused. Of course, anything you don't understand, always ask for an explanation or an example, and don't be intimidated by not understanding it at the outset.

The Balance Sheet

The balance sheet (now often called the statement of financial position) is the document which shows your assets – the items worth money – and your liabilities – what you owe.

A cashflow forecast will highlight whether you will have enough cash to pay your bills or whether you might need funding at certain stages of the year. Unless you are good on financial jargon, insist everything is explained to you in a manner that you understand.

Keep asking, get to the important aspect, get to the significant part. Bankers, accountants and financial advisors all have their own jargon and sometimes hide behind it or don't want to explain what the document means in plain language – keep asking the questions until you are happy. Make money work for you and be a jargon buster.

Remember – it is your money and your financial opportunity. Get past the jargon and get to the opportunity. Keep it simple for yourself. The main people to beware of are those selling you financial products. Take charge and use your resilience and capability to stay in control.

Using Technology

Modern technology should allow you to keep track of things so much more effectively and faster.

Keep asking questions, never leave a meeting or sign anything until you are clear about what is going on and the implications for you. If you think it's necessary, get a second opinion. There is no need to be a banker or an accountant to achieve financial or business success, just have a clear understanding of what your needs are. With the right attitude you can make this happen. Money and handling it is part of your life.

Use your apps to keep track of your bank account and your tax situation and try to keep building your financial knowledge.

Profitability, cash flow and net worth are important terms. Profitability measures whether any business side hustle is making more money than its running costs, so you know not to waste your time on a side hustle that isn't profitable.

Cash flow measures the timing of money in and out. Are there times in the month that you are close to running out of money in your account? Watch your cash flow at that crucial time. When cash is plentiful, and you are more relaxed, be aware of the potential to spend unnecessarily.

Net worth is whether you are owed more or have items worth more money than your debts. Ultimately this is something you want to build up.

It can be a bit overwhelming to take all this on board at once if you are young. Break it into straightforward steps for yourself stage by stage.

Build Financial Habits

What you do every day, every week, will ultimately affect how you perform financially. Handling your finances well will give you a good money mindset and keep you from worrying needlessly. It can create financial freedom and reduce the stress surrounding finances.

By the time you reach midlife it may be too late to create anything significant for the future, which is why if you can be strategic and plan a little now, you will certainly reap the benefits later. Building compound interest and the power that long-term investment brings will improve your financial situation.

What are the good financial habits that matter and will bring you significant long-term results without impinging too much on your everyday lifestyle?

1. Learn to understand finance to make it worthwhile. Find the balance between short-term and long-term gratification. Make your money work for you, meeting your needs now and for the future.

2. How can the other seven E Factors help your financial success?

    They will make an enormous difference and used together will get you the best short-term and long-term results. (This is something we will study later in the book, bringing together all the competencies to achieve goals.)

    Each has an impact on each other and work best as a set of skills. Personally, during my career I was successful and winning many awards. I am the only professor who has been awarded the OBE for Enterprise Education. There are additional awards and endorsements for my work, which all sounds great, and I am grateful for them all, but no extra income, or bonuses. I got lots of recognition and trophies but these do not pay for your upkeep. However, it can't all be measured in financial terms, you need both. My advice to you is achieve a balance of both.

I am blessed for what happened to me but on reflection, as your adviser and mentor, the cleverest thing for me to do would have been to have focused on both objectives. I am providing you with the best advice: using all the E Factors together will boost both your career and your financial well-being.

3. Use creativity to produce new business ideas and new products.

4. Use resilience to deal with anxiety over financial issues so you can make important decisions. The more relaxed and focused you are the better, and daily resilience practice allows you not to panic in short-term financial challenging situations.

5. Understand that your profile on and offline has financial value short and long term for you. Use social media to reach influential people with your best profile and strong international connections. These all have a financial worth.

6. Show leadership and build your advisers, investors and contacts into one team to create good connections and constructive interaction. This will be worth money to you.

7. Strategic thinking is vital, you must see the big picture and stay updated on market trends and influencers. You need to stay well informed and keep updating and growing your network. Spot the opportunities and be ready to act, and where possible invest for the long term.

8. Using your negotiation skills to do the right deals and your personal influence skills to sell projects, and get investment and opportunities will prove successful.

Hopefully, this shows how each of the competencies are not isolated, and if you can link them up and use them together, they will enhance financial and career results.

Of course, in this area your financial habits are the crucial ones, but the power of the model is bringing the E Factors together for maximum impact short or long term.

This is why you need to be competent in all eight E-Factor skills.

The Power of Leverage

What advantages, skills, contacts, or resources can you leverage? The word 'leverage' has been used in financial terms since 1933. So over 90 years later here we are still talking about it.

As you have seen there is no set formula – it's thinking ahead before each challenge and having solutions to put into place. Let's break it up, keep it simple.

Will I need a financial qualification?

The answer is: not necessarily. I was a qualified chartered accountant with financial planning certification from the Chartered Institute of Insurance. That may have given me significant financial literacy but harnessing the practical skills and authentic experience of others is equally beneficial.

Whatever situation, find your competitive advantage whatever that might be and use it.

Every challenge or opportunity has a different answer. Build all your E Factors and your confidence to highlight what can be done. One of the key things to remember is every situation has a financial implication short or long term. You need to find out what it is.

It is best not to be overly obsessed by money to the exclusion of building an entire project that is sustainable. Money will always play a key part whether it is the funding proposition, profitability measurement or asset development or protection.

Practical experience and learning from it is more important than professional qualification, though it is always useful when focusing on money and finance to have a variety of perspectives. Experience is always more valuable than qualifications provided you have learnt from the experiences.

The key is what do you want and what is your financial plan, short and long term. The most important thing is not to let any previous situation, good or bad, to influence you too much.

Funding

Any project that has potential to grow needs funding as the growth won't happen or could be risky without enough funding and the right type of funding.

Lending usually needs security, in the same way that a mortgage loan is tied to a house. Asset finance will be tied to assets and venture capital is taking a percentage of the company.

In small start-ups this is not usually an option early on unless the venture capitalist spots significant growth potential.

In many cases financing can be a mix of lending and equity investment. What is important is what additional resources, such as knowledge, expertise and experience, bring added value to equity investment.

Keep it simple.

Don't be baffled by financial terms or jargon. The key thing is to be prepared to understand a lot more even if you do not have to focus on it in whatever project you are involved with. It is common sense really and making use of whatever financial resources or advice that is available that could be beneficial for short- or long-term growth.

I am trying to encourage you to be streetwise about the financial aspects of any project. Even if you are at university or college the available funding is crucial.

In many cases the government will fund the preliminary stages of major projects in sectors such as education. For example, in the world of entrepreneurship education the UK government, through Gordon Brown, put significant funding in place for five years and then universities had to seek their own internal and external funding for the next stage.

The challenge comes in obtaining the sustainable funding for the next stage. The important thing to remember is get the initial project right and put things in place way ahead.

Finance is only one area, but it plays its part. Too often there is little funding for small start-ups who have the most limited access to money. If you start a new venture with serious potential for growth the funding will be limited to equity investors. These are the people who want a significant shareholding. It is not always easy to get because usually significant financing is needed to bring in management and get the company up and running.

Other projects will be smaller initially and only need minimal seed funding. Many small projects, run initially with only one or two people, get off the ground without any funding at all. Then either a challenge or an opportunity creates a pressure for finance for growth. It's difficult to get either equity or lending finance at this stage and that is where the local sector, such as a regional development agency, can step in.

The knowledge you learn tells you that money plays a big part in all ventures at any stage and in any sector. The handling of any money in a new venture is crucial, as part-time ventures can easily run out of funding very quickly. In addition to regional support, look for public sector funding of start-ups, which will be regularly available from the local enterprise centre.

Employee Financing

We have covered the various financial aspects of starting a venture and making projects happen within an organisation. If you're working within an existing private company or in the public sector it is important, if the project is to happen, that you have access to a budget.

There will usually be a financial appraisal project and usually any new project won't be allowed to begin until early funding has been confirmed. Again, this is where it is important to use all the E Factors within the organisation to get the project funded, to make it happen and to meet internal and regional objectives. The public sector is vastly different from the private sector, and so is the community sector.

An important thing to do is your strategic research within your organisation and understand senior management priorities. Trying to be entrepreneurial within the public sector you will need all the E-Factor skills. Use them to achieve your objectives within the public sector context. Getting your message out to people who not only understand how their public sector organisation has worked but can help you navigate the internal system.

Now you will need to be innovative but within the context of the organisation. Getting budgets, showing outcomes for projects, and carrying out risk assessments are vital to meet public sector accountability objectives.

It is different and has advantages and disadvantages in comparison to the private sector. There is a clear need for innovative executives to take the public sector into the 21st century.

Finding that internal mentor who can help you navigate the system is crucial. Be clear what your objectives are and work within the system. Budgets and accountability are arguably even more important in the public sector. I have used the E-Factor system within several universities successfully. This works very well if you research your organisation, link to its objectives and follow all procedures while still being innovative.

Being an intrapreneur can be equally as rewarding as working in the private sector. Wherever you work, you must fit into the system and its ethos whilst using your E-Factor skills. The E-Factor skills are relevant to both private and public sector and indeed the third sector.

Technology affects every type of organisation and every region. The financial skills, reporting systems and accountability will vary slightly depending on the system favoured by that organisation. Your key objective must be to be adaptable and achieve high impact. Learn the E Factor and develop an understanding of your own organisation formally and informally – then you can be confident and have impact.

Your Financial Plan

As discussed, finance is a crucial element in life in general and throughout all organisations. You can learn financial skills and you can learn the E Factor, which can be used in any type of institution.

A sound generic grounding in finance will support you and when you find your project look at the organisational context. How can you use the E Factor and achieve the financial objectives targeted within your organisation? As the 21st century unfolds, and artificial intelligence (AI) increases in popularity, organisations need to become more efficient and effective and people need to be prepared to instigate change whilst working within the protocols and systems of whatever public or private sector organisation they work for. There is an incredible opportunity if you get the financial and systems side right and yet achieve the innovation objectives. The E Factor can make it happen.

Advice for You

Learn to understand and respect money in whatever context you are in. Appreciate, develop and understand your E-Factor skills, acknowledge and accept your chosen type of organisation so you can make impactful sustainable change. Where would you prefer to work? What do you want to achieve and what resources do you need? Every type of organisation needs your skillset, your talents and adaptability. Find your opportunity to make it happen and go for it!!

Chapter 3

Creativity

Creativity is your ability to think creatively and to make connections between different things to create a new and innovative solution.

You use the right side of the brain to do this as many problems or challenges cannot be solved by logical analysis, which traditional education encourages.

Creativity tends to be encouraged and taught in education and home life up to age eleven. Then in teen years, school creativity all but disappears from the curriculum, usually being only taught in subjects outside the mainstream like art or music. What this means is that you end up creating a future workforce who can analyse challenges but are unable to create new or innovative solutions to problems. The irony is that in the Fourth Industrial Revolution logical analysis can be provided by bots and computers but with a distinct lack of innovative solutions to latest problems often on a global scale. Creativity is something you personally need if you are to prosper and be successful in the global economy.

To increase or develop your creativity you need to rekindle your child-like qualities, be curious, use your imagination and keep an open mind. Go to places you normally wouldn't dream of going, to become more adventurous.

Creativity needs to be taught to everyone. Not only to those in education but to the entire working population. It is the key skill that differentiates a person from a machine, and which drives and underpins innovation.

Unless you continue to study subjects such as art, music, media, design and so on, the right side of the brain will not be used to its full capacity from age twelve, and you will lose the capability to think creatively.

Creativity is one of the important E Factors and without it you will struggle to deal with change and to make the most of any opportunities that arise.

It is now recognised at the highest level that creativity is the underpinning skill and the catalyst for survival in the global economy. It will take time to change the education system to take this into account so you must take personal responsibility to reclaim and restore your own creative potential and that of others. Go for it! The age of artificial intelligence demands it and is challenging you.

I hope you are convinced that creativity is vital and the keystone of innovation.

Innovation occurs constantly and will increase significantly at all levels in the next few years. Will you be ready, and will you continue to evolve in the light of further changes?

How can you improve and help others to do the same? The answer is to adopt and observe the habits that creative people have and encourage your colleagues to do the same. It is never too late. Machines have been and will continue to be the key focus. Remember, it is your individual skills and competencies that will enable you to take projects forward and make a difference.

Where to start. Let us do the creativity and innovation test now!

Answer the following questions:

- Have you ever drafted a story or painted a picture?
- Have you ever dared to dream or imagine connections between different subjects and countries?
- Are you willing to experiment and take risks?
- How unique are your ideas?

These may not be things you have thought of recently, but I'd bet at some time you have.

It is time to recapture or even re-invent those key skills and use them to achieve your goals and make a difference.

If you can do it, you can then inspire others, and achieve more within your community or company.

The first thing is to admit the truth. Do you accept you now live in a global economy where you will compete for jobs on an international basis and have the potential to be a global leader? You need to be honest with yourself and take responsibility for your own development. Know your potential, understand your uniqueness – that's what makes you stand out.

First Step

Be curious. Remember when you were interested in everything and were open to the latest ideas and change – what happened?

Unfortunately, traditional education is focused solely on left brain thinking but does not consider personal development. Gordon Brown as Chancellor of the Exchequer in 2002 funded lecturers and trainers to go to Boston to the famous Massachusetts Institute of Technology, where there had been several remarkably successful technological start-ups.

It was a great idea to open our minds in February 2002, but we received no teaching in innovation or practical enterprise skills. It is fun to brainstorm with others and to be outrageous in your strategies and solutions and it is where the biggest learning and development will happen.

Begin to use your imagination and both sides of your brain to ensure you make the greatest impact. If you can't get support or find an opportunity from your own organisation, take charge, and find examples and games and re-learn. It is time for you to get curious again. Become interested in everything and not just in that which is directly relevant to you. If you have not played sport for years, then try something new. If you are not a sporty person look around and find something you are interested in and try it. If you have dreamed of visiting another country, research all about it and produce activities and plans of what you could do when you go there. Opportunities are around you, but you must actively look for them.

Curiosity is the key thing. You need to understand how the world works not only within your own subject area or geographic location but also in the big, exciting, often intimidating, world.

Set yourself some creativity goals now.

I hope my plea for a change in your mindset and attitude is working.

This is so important. You need to recapture and begin to use both sides of your brain.

It's never too late. I once trained over five hundred Chinese executives in creativity in a day. This was at the University of Cambridge. They came prepared to trust me to try the creative exercises and they had fun. There were many brilliant ideas created on that sunny afternoon. Let's not forget to have fun along the way. It worked for the Chinese executives who had previously no experience of creativity. It can work for you.

Perhaps the most important thing is to be open minded and relaxed. Be prepared to have some fun and you will be surprised at the results.

This was what I learned when I introduced creativity into the enterprise curriculum about fifteen years ago.

I faced a rather challenging situation but one which taught me a lot and helped me confirm the power of creativity.

I was already doing some creativity exercises with business students and had a reputation for lecturing in an innovative way.

As part of a social enterprise initiative, once a year Queens University brought a range of teenagers into the university for a day. Most of these young teens were not interested in their education, preferring to skip school for other outdoor activities.

I informed them about university opportunities, which could include them. Their main lecture was on creativity, as my classes in this area had all gone down well. Little did I know what I was letting myself in for and what I would learn from the experience!

I did my usual fun exercises, but the class acted disruptively and found the exercises tedious. This was something alien to me, and I worried that these teens might just get up and walk out. It was all getting extremely uncomfortable.

I tried to think of something that might solve the situation. I asked them could they help me with a challenge. I needed to walk my dog every morning before coming into work, but it was getting so much harder with the cold dark mornings, what could I do? Everyone was quiet for a moment.

Then one lad spoke out and said, 'why don't you buy your dog a treadmill? Put him on it every morning, and yourself. You look like you could use the exercise.' He laughed and so did the rest of the class.

We continued producing ridiculous ideas for other pets until the class ended. However, it taught me a lesson about creativity. A month or two later I was watching the BBC program *Dragons Den* where entrepreneurs get a chance to pitch their business ideas to famous businesspeople to raise money. One young entrepreneur pitched her idea, which was – yes, a doggie treadmill.

She was successfully funded and became a tremendous success around the world. I never heard from my disruptive visitor again, but I wonder if he ever knew that by making that outrageous suggestion, he could have produced a million-pound idea!

Keep making those outrageous suggestions and be curious, sometimes ridiculous and you never know what you could create.

That true story highlights that there are all sorts of opportunities out there, not only to create products but to learn and make things happen in the 21st century. Listen to everyone's ideas, and then explore the significance of them. It is a clear survival skill in the 21st century.

Richard Branson, himself a great innovator, will confirm curiosity to be the number one skill.

Become interested in everything around you, look to see how it can be improved, and embrace any changes. Researchers have found that curiosity prepares the brain for learning. If you can keep interested in your area of work, you will achieve more. I would encourage you to set your intention to become a lifelong learner.

Travel as much as you can, for you will learn so much about different countries and diverse cultures, which can foster a vast range of innovative ideas.

It is important for us all to observe and anticipate innovative technologies and the opportunities they provide. Don't limit yourself to one area – so many new products and services originate from mixing products from various locations. The doggie treadmill outlined earlier is a splendid example of this. No matter what disruption appears, it is an opportunity for someone to create novel solutions and new products.

As with all creative skills observe those who you admire, who are successful and replicate where appropriate. I don't mean copy their product or service but more how they behave and respond in different scenarios.

Converse with a range of people and be interested in what they are saying. You will learn about alternative approaches and ideas. Eventually, you will find the right idea.

Creativity is one of the key E Factors you should try to practise every day. Keep that open mind and be interested in everything. Eventually, you will make the connection between different ideas that will create an innovation. Go for it!

There is a power in connecting disparate ideas and challenges that can create an answer to a problem. You are always looking for the latest opportunities.

Divergent thinking is vital. It may initially be challenging to do but persevere.

Set aside some time each day if you can make connections, or brainstorm with colleagues. The more you explore new areas the more potential opportunities you will have to contribute.

What is amazing is how much useful information is readily available. You must combine your creativity with the capacity to assess what is more likely to work. Be a team player. Your connections are vital and social media gives you the opportunity to develop this. Help others often and many will return the favour and help you.

If someone has a problem there could be an opportunity for your product or service to help them, or to send them useful referrals. This is how I initially produced the E Factor. I was looking for a book which would help my students do some innovation or entrepreneurship work. I couldn't find one, so I wrote my own.

There is an identified opportunity to helping people succeed and grow during the Fourth Industrial Revolution. At present there is no identified answer and the E Factor provides a solution.

Daily Activity

Using these skills requires daily activity, to develop the habit and never take it for granted. Every day is a learning day, and you must practise your E-Factor competencies daily to be as good as you can. The one lesson I hope you have picked up is that there is significant difference between knowing what you should do and implementing it.

You have to be honest with yourself and continually obtain outside feedback. Making these habits part of your day will ensure you achieve your goals and help others.

Keep a journal and self-assess and get third-party opinions where possible. Every day should be a learning day and a practice day. Creativity is one important E Factor. The other seven E-Factor competencies help you to turn the creativity from idea into reality.

Create a culture of learning creativity and action. At the start of every day, review your plan. Write up your journal at the end of every day to keep yourself accountable and keep learning!

Embed structures and processes into your work to ensure creativity happens.

You must learn from any mistakes and get honest and trusted third-party feedback, to keep improving on your ideas. You may be a small or large organisation – that does not matter. What matters is that you have systems in place which will assist you should things go wrong.

You and your team should live creativity every day and keep pushing yourself to improve. This is how you will reap the benefits from being creative.

Daily habits should be linked to a monthly review. It's why you should get some type of external coach. One who doesn't work for you and who will once a month ask you challenging questions. It is surprising how many successful people have an external coach. Reciprocate if you can by offering your time and your skills to local charities or schools who could benefit from your experience.

Do not lose your creativity no matter what your success to date. Be available for your creativity practices and keep your skills and knowledge up to date.

Stay grounded, and you will learn something new each day. All eight E Factors are needed for success and arguably creativity is the key to identifying new opportunities of all kinds. For this to happen you need to be a resilient learner and keep searching to improve your brand, manage your team and think ahead.

Appreciate your success but understand that without constant practice you could very easily lose the skills that have got results to date. Find ways to challenge yourself and find people who will give you honest feedback whatever you do. One example, while at Queens University I failed to get a grant I applied for. I sought feedback and I got a very honest reply, which made an impact. It appeared I didn't complete the application form fully. I was informed 'complete the application 100 per cent or don't bother wasting people's time'. Learn to give 100 per cent – anything less is a waste of your time.

What activity could you do daily which would allow your creativity to remain strong? Think of a few useful ideas which you wouldn't normally do and try them out.

Meet other creatives from other areas and model them. What can you learn from the most unexpected sources? Can you be creative with your time? Meet and help creatives who have had failure. There is much to learn from those who have been unsuccessful at times. Learn what they did wrong and how they salvaged the situation.

Most importantly remember that creativity is one of your greatest tools. Look after it well and use it every day to increase its potential.

Chapter 4

Negotiation

Your ability to negotiate successfully will play a significant part in your career success. As the son of a car dealer, you think I would have been a natural in this area, but I was busy taking traditional academic exams at school and university and did not realise what a vital skill it is.

A few years into my career I realised that without negotiation I was allowing myself to get a poor reward for my efforts. I had to work at it, but I am glad I did as the deals I can negotiate and my achievements in life have improved. You can only attain your short- and long-term objectives if you constantly practise negotiation skills and use them whenever you can.

Let me clarify. This is potentially the most important skill you need to be successful. Usually not taught at school or university, you need to learn it, use and constantly refine it – then you will enjoy the art of great deals. Learn, practise and use in real life situations and you will be good. With all the E Factors there are things to learn and apply. Rest assured you will still face negotiation situations and you may never become a world-class negotiator, but a level of competence can be achieved if you follow my advice and apply them to you and your team. Let's learn the theory and the practice now.

To begin, examine your level of competency you have now then plan a programme to change your dealmaking strategies. You will improve and learn to enjoy the process. Just understand what's involved in negotiation, practise and use it.

Everything is negotiable. Develop the skills and make it work for you. You will need to understand why the skills are necessary, and how to use them in your business and personal life. In common with the other E Factors, learn the skills, assess your present level, and then work on your development. It will pay dividends. Some of you may not feel comfortable with it initially. Some of you have been doing deals since kindergarten.

Let's look at what you need.

Background and Lessons

I am sharing a little of my own background. I learned the lesson that if you find what someone wants, are clear about your own objectives and reach a compromise this can work well.

I was fortunate to watch my father, a car salesperson, doing deals nearly every day, as he worked from home. It took me a long time to understand what the skills were that he was using.

I gradually understood that the result of a negotiation was not down to luck but to being the most effective dealmaker.

Everyone must develop their own style of negotiation for the situation they are in. It takes time to get the principles together and make them part of your communication style. Some of you may think it is just a matter of bringing in an experienced negotiator on your behalf, but even though professional help can be useful at times, you will still need to develop your own style and strategies that work for you and the situations you face.

I thought only car dealers like my father did deals and negotiated prices, and no one else did. I thought the more qualifications I had, then doing deals wouldn't matter. I could not have been more wrong.

You will use these skills in your personal, business and professional life. You will do them face to face, online or by phone. It is a lifelong skill that will always be useful no matter what you do. If you don't negotiate skilfully, you will have to accept whatever someone gives you and quite often it won't be anywhere near the deal you really wanted. That is the reality, it is an art and a science so let's learn it, because nearly everything is negotiable!

What Are the Skills?

There are a clear set of skills that you must learn for each stage of negotiating a potential deal. The following questions will help:

1. What do you want? What is the minimum you need to achieve in any transaction?

2. What is the best venue for the negotiation and how can you adapt to the circumstances?
3. What information is needed before the meeting?
4. Do you need specialist support?
5. What research can you do?
6. Can it be a win–win negotiation?
7. How can you seek to understand the position of the other party, before communicating your own position?
8. What have previous deals taught you?
9. How can you practise beforehand?
10. Can you walk away if you don't feel you have a fair deal?

Every deal you negotiate will teach you a valuable lesson about yourself and the other party. You must learn the lesson, good or unfair, but also learn to enjoy the process no matter what.

Let me show you a method that worked for me when I negotiated with a university and the stages I went through to get a strong long-term deal. Like all deals it was not perfect, but a good long-term deal was achieved by both parties.

First, I did my research on the university and the people involved.

I prepared some questions for the meeting, which would ensure I knew what was important to them. I found out they liked my practical background and were impressed with my awards. I understood they wanted me to bring something new to the university.

I had to give a fifteen-minute presentation, so I did a trial run by visualising the scene, practising my presentation and getting feedback from three different people.

At the meeting, I listened. I asked my questions and began to understand their position. I built rapport.

I was clear about what I could accept and communicated that.

I took notes and followed up with a written communication after the meeting.

Next came an online meeting where they were happy with my presentation, I was happy with their offer, and the deal was done.

That may sound a little easy but there were some tough discussions during the meeting. One of the key things that helped me was I practised my presentation a number of times before with someone who did their best to challenge and to question me on my decisions and choices.

I went through the process and so did they. I also noticed some things I could have done differently but I knew what I was prepared to accept and what I wasn't. Sometimes, though, despite your best effort the deal is not right, and you must be prepared to walk away.

I am not a natural negotiator, some people are. I had to break the process down and do it a step at a time. I had to refine and improve my communication skills, and I showed respect during the process and understood where the other party was coming from.

You are always aiming for a win–win position where possible.

Some potential deals you will notice right away won't work and will create havoc, or disruption and so you must walk away regardless of the potential short-term gain. This will become one of your strengths, the ability to walk away when your gut tells you this is not a good deal.

If you negotiate well, you will protect yourself and your projects.

Your ability to identify potential risk in a deal and walk away where appropriate will be important for your long-term survival and development.

The Qualities of Great Negotiators

Please don't try and copy someone else's style. Learn their strategies, but be your own person and do things your way.

Always aim for the deal that is sustainable. The more deals you do the more lessons you will learn. Every transaction is a learning one.

Some people love doing deals and some find them difficult and uncomfortable.

Using the other seven E-Factor competencies will help you to negotiate a good deal.

Can you create innovation solutions that work for both parties? Are you resilient? Does your physical and mental health keep you strong? Do you learn from every negotiation?

If you do, you will be able to spot challenges and opportunities early on before a deal is completed.

Are you persuasive, charismatic or manipulative?

Do you view each negotiation as a learning experience, something you might grow to enjoy? Like all the skills some people will have a natural flair or background which lends itself easily to the negotiation environment.

Use the process, find your own style and where necessary call on others to help you through the most difficult parts.

Always try to give the other side a fair deal as this will build your reputation for future deals. How you leave negotiations will become your trademark. Document the experience, the advantages, and disadvantages. Are you strategic in building long-term potential as well as achieving short-term solutions?

You will remember the great deals, and the not so great – document them all. Some will be easier than others – you want to learn and improve from each one.

Negotiation is an art as well as a science. All eight E Factors are important but it's the deals you do that will ensure your survival and capacity to thrive long term.

Master this skill and change your life and that of others.

Chapter 5

Personal Branding

You need to make people aware of your work and your profile in this technological age.

The important thing is to do good work and ensure others know about it.

Your profile will reflect who you are and what you do, where you do it, and who you are hoping to attract. Sounds a bit like a dating site doesn't it? Think about whose attention you are trying to attract.

Be professional, be yourself and know which market you are aiming for and help that market to find you. Then you can help them, by showing examples on your profile of how you have been successful, how you have solved issues and gained a good reputation.

Talk about your expertise, your qualities, and skills. It is an extremely competitive market out there. You need to stand out and be noticed in a positive way. Personal branding is a game changer.

The benefit of positive personal branding is it gives you leverage when you come to negotiate for your salary, or for a promotion.

Identify your unique skills, and highlight them. People who view your profile will want to see the positive part of you, keep it professional.

Protect yourself – online trolling and trashing can happen to anyone, be aware. Your confidence can be easily shattered by jealous remarks from others. It is best not to retaliate or comment back on an open forum.

Personal branding should help you to get clarity about what you want to achieve, what you aspire to and keep your goals on track.

If you run a business, you need to find and keep interested customers. If you are an employee, you want to achieve your work objectives and get recognition and internal promotion.

Let's go through the process – what is the purpose of personal branding?

1. Be honest with yourself. Do you agree building your personal brand is important?
2. Be careful who you associate with. One of your greatest strengths will be the ability to build your brand and yet be yourself and don't change.
3. Identify your niche – what are you good at and what do you want to do? What do you want to achieve, and can you make it happen? Be clear who your target audience is.

4. Find the best platform or platforms to reach that audience.

5. Build a content strategy and build a consistent network and relationships.

6. Monitor, adapt and measure results.

7. Ensure all appropriate medias are being used.

Best Practice Examples

Gary Vaynerchuk, Tony Robbins and Richard Branson are three well-known examples of people who have created extraordinarily successful high-impact brands.

You may initially have more modest goals than those entrepreneurs, but you can learn from them and others. Eventually you will find what works for you. I do think it is good to have a specific niche and understand who your target audience is and reach them with a compelling message.

The Key Benefits of Personal Branding

The benefits include enhancing your visibility, expanding your opportunities for work and collaboration and perhaps most importantly of all you will constantly be highlighting your unique contribution to your chosen niche.

Accept that you must build your brand rather than wait to be discovered.

If you are running a business, that is a powerful personal marketing tool. You will need a mix of activities that will build your personal brand.

What four things are you going to try over the next six months?

A Sample Plan

Ask yourself:

1. What do I want to achieve here? Can I also benefit my community and employer?
2. What social enterprise could help me while building my personal brand?
3. What causes do I care about? How can I help?
4. What is my chosen mix of social media? What content will I have online that will be unique and positive?

Video, speeches, articles and podcasts can all work, but your own personal branding plan will depend on what you are trying to achieve.

When building your brand, you need to apply the other E Factors also, to attain a greater impact and chances of sustained success. Let's get branding.

My Experience

I have been successful at getting my personal brand, and my work, recognised nationally and internationally. I began with making others aware of what I was doing and offering those who were struggling to implement enterprise education a helping hand. This is also how you learn and gain experience. Something you need to be clear about is what you really want to achieve.

Always ask those who you trust for honest feedback. At times this can be difficult to accept but will allow you to change and adapt at each stage if necessary.

Keep reviewing your performance and the correct mix of personal marketing activity. All should yield short- and long-term results.

A good definition of personal branding is: 'Your skills, experience, personality traits and values.'

We must highlight our own unique mix of skills and experiences. Be authentic and truthful, and clearly highlight what you can do to help others. Be clear and confident about your own impact. Then get your message out there and seek opportunities.

Be systematic. All your personal branding work should focus on the five C's: clarity, consistency, content, confidence and commitment.

Know your objectives and use your skills and strategies to achieve them. Don't expect instant success – it takes time to build up something worthwhile.

Engage and build relationships not just with customers but other key influencers. Try to contribute something unasked first, to increase your chances of getting reciprocation.

There will be considerable benefits if you stick with this agenda.

Eventually some significant business or industry people will support your work and refer other people to it at an early stage. If you are systematic and keep learning it will happen. It is good to sell your potential products and services at a competitive price but include outstanding service as part of the package.

The Benefits

When you get it right, you will potentially build a good network early on, so you will attract more clients at a premium price and a strong platform to operate from.

If your personal brand is seen as authentic that will boost its value. You will have to be adaptable and be a lifelong learner.

You must work to get that break that will eventually come if you keep moving forward. Patience and adaptability need to be strong qualities at this stage.

It can be tempting just to go ahead regardless of any feedback, but any consistent feedback is giving you a lesson to save and develop your business. Make your business plan and be clear what you want both short and long term. Here are some of the questions your potential network will be seeking clarification on:

1. What are your skills?
2. What key benefit do you bring others?
3. Is your personal brand credible and sustainable?
4. What is your vision?
5. Do you have a mission and a value proposition?

In the world today we are all in such a rush to make things happen that we do not welcome any setbacks that may slow us down even in the short term. It is why you need to plan strategically and retain funding for any innovations needed.

Keep learning, keep innovating and the opportunities will come. It is understandable we all want instant success but is that realistic? You or your business may have exciting potential, but you will need to be patient and resilient.

Co-Branding

You can link to other good brands through working with them or for them. When I moved to Queens University, Belfast, which has an exceptionally excellent quality brand, it strengthened my own personal brand. I worked for Cambridge, another strong branded university, which also enhanced my branding.

Winning over forty-five national and international awards for my enterprise education and the E Factor allows me great opportunities to co-brand. The co-branding with the Times Higher Education awards and USASBE (the United States Association for Small Business and Entrepreneurship) have also been helpful. What you will find as someone starting up, if you ask politely for help from successful people who started out in the same way, they are often keen to mentor or assist when they can because they understand your position.

Writing and speaking can be especially useful for your brand, particularly if linked to social media at each stage. Ask for assistance and support – you may not be discovered overnight but you could be surprised who will help you and respond to your requests.

Be a Warrior

Have a variety of strategies to promote your personal brand. Use about five or six strategies together and be consistent. Persist and learn and you will get your break. Be sincere, honest and relaxed when things don't seem to be happening at the pace you want. Help others when you can and take consistent action.

Anything is possible. Be creative, get your message out in non-expensive ways – even to those who you think may not be interested. People talk, they like to discuss new things, new projects. Be one of those new opportunities people talk about. I believe you will be surprised at the results! Go for it.

The key thing is to find the right personal brand that fits in with you and your beliefs.

Put yourself and what you have to offer out there, all the time. People will help you because of your honesty and integrity and your desire to have impact. Draw up a personal branding plan, ask for help and implement. Your skills and contacts and profile will keep improving.

Stay relaxed – it's a numbers game. Focus on your plan and what you want to achieve, and the universe will move things around and open opportunities for you. Take them and learn from them and help others when you can. We all know about the law of attraction and the law of Karma. In business marketing and personal branding you will get more opportunities because you helped others. Allow your personal brand to shine, all the time.

Chapter 6

Strategic Thinking

Y̶ou need to learn strategic thinking skills. It is of course important to take one day at a time, but just as vital to anticipate risk and recognise opportunities. One of my key memories as a newly qualified accountant was getting information highlighting trends and results that were identified for the next ten years and ignoring it, with the view that it was not relevant to me now.

The strategic predictions came true, and I faced some challenges as I was not prepared for the predicted changes in trends and opportunities. It is of course always good to be prepared to take care of business in the here and now. However, being prepared for the future is also good, and you can minimise any risks involved. Obviously, senior management people focus on the long term but you or your business are unlikely to do anything significant unless you know the trends, the likely opportunities and pitfalls and are prepared.

I have every sympathy for people who will not or cannot look ahead, perhaps because of an immediate challenge. However, if you do not plan, you will not be prepared for the changes that inevitably happen. For instance, as I pointed out earlier, we are in the Fourth Industrial Revolution. What does that mean? It means you need new skills and a new mindset to be ready for the challenges and opportunities that artificial intelligence will bring. Either be prepared strategically or accept the consequences. The good news is that you are in the right place reading this book. Before we go into the specific skills of strategic thinking, let me highlight some of the key qualities that a good strategic thinker has, which will work to your advantage short and long term:

- They always learn and listen to others who have researched strategic trends.
- They never forget the strategic aims of their organisation and business.
- They keep up to date with news and trends.

Adding strategic thinking and taking action means you will be more likely to create sustainable opportunities and results rather than short-term gains.

The key lesson to learn is that strategic thinking should underpin the other seven critical E-Factor skills. Let's take two simple examples to illustrate this.

- *Finance.* Too often we do not plan where we want to be financially over a lengthy period. You need to think strategically where you want to be financially and set up a system to invest money over a mid-term period. Sounds a little boring to some of you, I know, but I have seen too many people make a lot of money short term, spend it, then struggle long term when profits or earnings are not available.

- *Personal branding.* It is good to develop short-term opportunities to get your brand out there but what is even more impressive is to use strategic thinking to carry out personal branding to create short and long-term brands, which in turn will create competitive advantage for you. It takes time to build anything good and you must use your strategic thinking to build something that will last and work over the medium or long term.

Always ask yourself, where do you want to be in one, five or ten years?

Culture

Creating the right culture is important You may be a one-person company or one person in a larger company. Always be thinking ahead and planning the next five to ten years. One thing is for sure – the strategical planners always win long term. Do you want to win short and long term? I think you do. If not, I can only advise that you should. When practising any of the other E-Factor skills ask yourself every time: How can I be strategic as well as practical here?

It is vital to act on an ongoing basis to work towards your strategic plan. The key focus is to always get the balance between action and strategy.

Keep reviewing whether your actions are helping you to achieve both short- and long-term goals. Determination to keep going is good but you may have to adjust the strategies if they are not working. Have a clear mission statement. Being passionate about what you do is also important. Self-assessment is good, but you also need outside feedback.

Do you have a vision, and have you broken it down into goals to create a series of steps? Strategy for the long term is crucial – you need to take steps and receive external feedback alongside your own thoughts on where you are at now and where you are going.

Find your niche and build to achieve your short- and long-term goals.

It is just as important not only to have a long-term strategy but also early identification of obstacles you might meet along the way. It's the skills you acquire on your strategic journey that will help you long term in life.

Useful Steps to Take

Draw up a five-year strategic plan and a one-year business plan. Create a weekly activity chart. Act, review and keep learning.

Step by step plan your mission. Be clear on what it is you wish to achieve. Where are you now and where do you wish to be? Focus on your goals and anticipate problems when you can. Understand you have a life purpose which motivates you but there are likely to be challenges along the way that will require innovative thinking.

Be excited by the person you are becoming on your journey through learning and developing, which will give you a model to teach others. In achieving this you will develop and hone skills that you can use in a variety of projects and have new capabilities.

Learn to balance short-term and long-term goals. Breaking down every step is fine, but it is vital to keep that focus for a wide range of situations. It is likely you will face both major and minor challenges, some of which you may not overcome first time round. No matter how accomplished you already are always welcome the learning, even from short-term set-backs. It won't matter how successful you have been to date you will face challenges and get new learning experiences. It is this thirst to learn, particularly from short- and long-term setbacks, that will shape your strategic future and create further successful opportunities. Link your strategic plan to short-term action plans to turn a good plan into reality.

There are several good models that will help you. The most practical one is the 'balanced scorecard'. It focuses on four main areas and if you keep on top of all four it increases your chances of becoming successful. The areas are: learning and growth, business processes, customers and finance.

If you use this model and stay in control of these four distinct areas it sets an effective strategy and links it to daily action.

One lesson to learn is to set aside some time each week to keep an eye on long-term trends and any need for short-term action, should you need to turn things around. Make this a regular habit and it will be of benefit long term. Dr Stephen Covey, in his excellent book *The Seven Habits of Highly Effective People*, reminds us of the importance of strategic thinking through ensuring that you always do important work and not focus 100 per cent on urgent short-term activity.

Creating the self-discipline to do this has incalculable benefits, including minimising both short-term and long-term risk.

Seek out successful people to learn from. If you find someone who has been successful for a sustained period, learn from them. These people will be highly effective and good at managing their day and time. You need to model their behaviour and find a way to make some of their strategies your own. The strategic thinker anticipates challenges and finds a way to achieve short-term goals on the way to long-term strategic success.

It is not easy to focus on short-term and long-term implications at the same time, but they must be linked, or you are in trouble. It is the main reason many new ventures do not last even if they started well. It is not easy to think ahead when you already have challenging short-term projects. All the eight E Factors are interlinked, and you need them all in working order to achieve a positive result – your creativity, resilience, personal influence and negotiation skills will all play a part.

Chapter 7

Leadership

Leadership is another important skill to accomplish. This is your capacity to make projects happen, working with teams and resources to create tactical and strategic advantage. It is essential not only in business but in every area of life.

It is the capacity to bring out the best qualities in others as well as yourself to attain your stated objectives. Leadership applies to every area of society, from large companies and public sector organisations to small businesses and social enterprises. There are no models which guarantee success as every situation and organisational structure is different.

The ability to inspire, to learn from setbacks and make projects sustainable is needed, together with adequate human and financial resources. Some people believe that certain people are born leaders. In reality there are a host of factors which account for the success of any leader.

Learn these, make them part of your own skill base, and then make it happen, whatever the circumstances or situation.

One of the greatest attributes of any leader is the capability to inspire people to adapt to circumstances and achieve results, whatever the challenge. There are many skills to learn but the first thing is to have a strategic vision that is accepted by all key players, and then the competence to implement it successfully.

Leaders will all have distinctive styles and different challenges to face, but there are key competencies they all must attain, which will be the major components of successful project completion.

You may not visualise yourself as a leader, but you have the potential to be one. You will have your own style based on your character and background and the key leadership trait you need is the drive to achieve results with the help of people and resources.

There are no techniques we must all adopt but becoming a lifelong learner and flexible in situations is a great leadership skill.

Develop the skills and mindset and then apply them in an industry you want to work in.

Begin with the focus on self-leadership.

Build your leadership competencies before you take on the leadership role required. Ideally, you want to lead in an industry or work area that motivates you – creating a sense of purpose and working in an area you are passionate about. If you show this as a leader, you are likely to share this with your team, no matter how big or small.

Self-awareness is very important. Understand what you are good at. Are your behaviours consistent? Are you a good decision maker? Do you make good choices? No matter your achievements we continue to be a work in progress. If you are unsure in any of these areas, ask others for their evaluation of you.

Build your confidence. For every problem or set back, there is always a solution, and you will find it. Remaining calm in demanding situations is important not only for you, but it will have a direct effect on the teams and individuals who you lead or influence.

How confident you appear carries considerable weight. Communicate clearly and effectively with authority the direction of the company.

Keep working on and demonstrate resilience as part of your leadership qualities.

Continue to work on and improve your own mental and physical health. This will help you to inspire well-being and confidence. You will need strength in these areas when something unexpected and challenging happens.

Not only must you be resilient, you must find a way of communicating this with impact to your team.

At times we can be placed in a leadership situation unexpectedly. This is a real test, and you must prepare for many situations. Your confidence under pressure will cascade through the organisation. This is the fundamental competency that will be an incredibly positive influence on the entire organisation.

Key Leadership Competencies

Influencing others is another key leadership skill. The main skills in this area include listening, which also includes picking up non-verbal cues, being non-judgemental and understanding other perspectives. Clarify what you just heard before offering any solutions and action steps to the key staff.

Your task, no matter how small or large your leadership group, is to empower others to achieve the specific goals they have been assigned.

Understand what motivates people and how you can create a team spirit. Delegation is important but everything you do and how you behave is crucial, as your core objective is to inspire confidence and teamwork no matter what the short-term challenges.

Preparation for Leadership

Should you not have an immediate opportunity to lead a team, it will help if you plan how you see yourself as a leader and try to get experience in motivating teams and leading projects, no matter how small. This could be for a charity or a local community group with limited funds.

It's a good place to practise your skills, see where you succeed and where you fall short and learn the lessons. Qualifications are useful, something like an MSc in Leadership with a practical basis. The underpinning research is helpful and some of it proves the efficacy of leadership skills. However, the more practical the course the better because writing a good assignment on leadership does not guarantee you can lead projects, people and teams on a pragmatic basis.

Challenge yourself and accept in the early days that you will be continually learning and repeating the process until you become confident with that skill.

Always be open minded and listen to people who have been there and come through it. They will offer you knowledge and expertise that will be especially useful.

Changing the Culture

You will set the culture in your actions and leadership style, making sure the culture is right for the organisation, the teams and the marketplace.

If the culture is not right for the company, the team and the business plan, you must change it, and you may require external help to do this.

It is important that key individuals play their part in setting the culture and you find a way of assessing if the cultural change is effective. Be proactive.

One cultural change is that you become a learning organisation. It does not mean that people need to do external courses but that senior staff demonstrate the willingness to learn new things and learn formally and informally and then teach the new strategies to their team.

People are always looking to model best practice and successful strategies. Change is never easy, and people need motivation and reward for embracing initiatives. It is amazing how positive or negative cultures can spread like wildfire so make sure it is a change for the better.

It is up to you to set the agenda and find ways of measuring performance at all levels.

Assess and get independent feedback to assess your credibility with internal and external key influencers. Learn from this and take appropriate action. In addition to making the big decisions you are setting the cultural norm. Get it right and there could be massive changes and opportunities ahead.

The Best Way to Learn Leadership

You are seeking the skills and mindset of the successful leader and yet you need to discover your own best style suitable for you and your leadership role.

Get started on a project you are interested in. Good leadership encompasses using all the E-Factor competencies yourself and encouraging other team members to model your behaviour. Acquire some coaching and get appraised regarding your own level, ideally from someone external to your potential chain of command. Work on yourself and set a good example for the rest of the team. Obtaining your first few successful leadership projects and finding your own unique style will determine if you are on the right path.

Finally, highlight the journey and the development steps needed to implement them. Where the team are on personal and management development programmes internally and externally, take part yourself to show you support them and that you have a commitment to lifelong learning like everyone else.

The Next Stage

Identify your deputy and future leaders at an early stage and build a strategic learning programme. Inspire, motivate and encourage as you highlight your plan and your leadership goals for the next few years. Be resourceful in helping your team feel valued and motivated and then find the appropriate learning and incentive schemes for them.

Your leadership style will be affected by your background, but keep learning and trying out what works best for you and you will inspire others to follow you. You will be judged on your initial handling of internal and external challenges. Be strong, detached and find a way to identify your future high-performing senior team members and a path for them to personally develop, achieve results and build their own teams.

Above all you want to encourage, show strength and a capacity to take corrective action where required. If you do this, you will find and develop your own successful team.

Continue identifying your own potential successor and give team members with potential the opportunity to make mistakes, learn and build their own teams for specific projects.

Living, breathing and demonstrating your core beliefs in your behaviour and decisions will provide clarity and inspiration at all levels. Creating a good team spirit is particularly important and you will need to get assistance to implement and use the most effective human resource development systems.

Your leadership challenges will depend on the company, existing culture and external opportunities and challenges.

Perhaps the most important thing is to recognise that everything you do sends out a message internally and externally. People like a strong but fair leadership style and if inspired you can gain significant traction and great loyalty.

Part of your role must go beyond achieving short- and long-term results. You are building a company that can operate effectively in the Fourth Industrial Revolution, where technology and artificial intelligence is bringing new challenges but a key focus on the right skills. You need to be an entrepreneurial leader who embraces innovation and both personal and corporate development.

You must set an example and keep learning and embracing opportunities. Get the culture right and have both the strategic and implementation plans in place.

Simultaneously identifying successors is vital. Leadership is more of an art than a science. Flexibility is key. Ultimately you will have to make the big decisions but what an opportunity to make an impact!

Chapter 8

Personal Influence

Who Needs to Influence Others?

We all need to communicate well, whatever our role. A student, an employee or anyone running a venture, will need to get people on their side and build healthy relationships at all levels.

An example from my own career. When I became an enterprise educator, my role was to introduce a new entrepreneurship curriculum into the timetable of Queens University, Belfast. They had used four years of a five-year funding package without achieving any results and I had a year to make it happen with little support. A bit of a challenge? You bet! I thought my job was to do some teaching but now it seemed

I had to make this project happen and persuade a wide range of stakeholders to take part and support it. These included people at all levels with a diversity of roles.

I used the full range of influencing skills to make it happen. I had face-to-face meetings with heads of department suggesting they allow me to do some work with a class in their department. I had to persuade students that learning to think like an entrepreneur was relevant and enjoyable and I somehow had to persuade senior management to give me more time than allocated.

At a few meetings, the head of department didn't even turn up. I had to report on my progress to the head of the university once a month. I used all my personal influencing skills to get people involved or at least less unsympathetic to this innovation. I learnt from all my failures that I needed to listen to the heads of departments and be relaxed about their lack of interest. I was relaxed about the initial rejections and kept improving my presentations. I listened attentively to the needs and concerns of the heads of departments and was respectful to one who had drafted a research paper showing that this particular project would never work.

Eventually I got my first breakthrough in the Environmental Planning department. I took action. I had to create a wonderful experience that the students would enjoy but also identify as relevant to the curriculum.

The range of stakeholders was breathtaking, and they all had to be influenced and persuaded in a unique way.

I got some initial success, and I knew if I could get some internal and external recognition for this work, it would broaden the scope and opportunity. The internal awards came shortly afterwards but I needed to get the work recognised externally to make an impact at a senior level. At this stage

I had been working closely with the UK enterprise education body. Then an opportunity came to apply for a national
teaching fellowship, which is the ultimate education award at
university level.

It was very tough getting shortlisted internally and completing my application to the Higher Education Academy
in England.

Like all good influencers I listened and got the support I
needed, submitted my application and it won the first ever
UK National Teaching Fellowship in enterprise education.

This changed everything and Queens University ended
up winning national and international awards for the enterprise work. After achieving this award, I received support at
the highest level internally and an abundance of external support. I share this to emphasise a few key learnings.

The skills of personal influencing are not just relevant to
someone who is involved in sales and marketing. It's something we all must do to make things happen in whatever area
in which you are involved. To gain support you need to communicate well with the range of stakeholders you deal with,
who all have different requirements.

You need to listen and learn. Then create a solution that
meets their needs. Even then your communication and listening skills must be used. The problems and opportunities
will continue to change, and you must learn and use all the
E-Factor skills to deliver.

Persuasion is different internally than selling or marketing
to an outside customer. Yet the fundamentals remain the same.
You probably learn more from your failures than your successes and the process never stops. Sharpen your own personal
influencing skills and develop your own style suitable for you
and your unique project.

Some people are amazed when they realise they need these skills in the corporate or public sector environment as well as in conventional business. The need is universal, but the skills need to be applied in a customised way in whatever sector or environment you work in.

The personal influence principles are always the same. Listen and understand first and identify and confirm what key stakeholders want or need. Get your message out professionally, internally and externally. Think both strategically and short-term gain.

A lot of the impact can be lost if integrity research or collaboration is ignored. My question to you is simple. You are now aware what influencing skills can do. Now how are you going to enhance yours and sustain them? Can you help others to do the same?

Underpinning your efforts to persuade others must be integrity and honesty. You are not trying to sell something without ethics. You are collaborating to achieve a good result in a professional and ethical way. You learn and get better after every project where experience will teach you strategic and tactical lessons.

Who are you going to influence in the next few months and how can you sustain it for mutual success and impact over the long term?

It is understood that in building personal influence you will have challenges. Try to enjoy the process, including your own faux pas and the disinterest of those who you are trying to influence.

Use a variety of mediums to communicate from and build a network and lead it. You can build global personal influence just by connecting different people and organisations. Build your influence and focus on contribution. You will be amazed at your impact if you build your networks and contacts by trying to help others.

Listen and learn. Then create a solution that meets their needs. Use all the E-Factor skills to deliver successfully.

You need to find your own influencing style and use it in an honest and appropriate way. You need to have clear strategies that work for you but always be aware where they are not working and prepare to be adaptable. You want to persuade people and, in some cases, you will be selling a project. Yet the most important thing is to really listen to what people are saying and understand their position first, before you attempt to present the best solution for them. People really appreciate genuine interest and someone who seeks clarity as to what you want and what your challenge or opportunity is. Research people and companies before you meet up and show genuine, not feigned, interest. It is very impactful with people but also appropriate behaviour. People really appreciate honesty and someone who does what they say they will do even if the situation has changed.

There is an immensely powerful influencing model known as NLP, or Neuro Linguistic Programming, devised in the 1970s by Bandler and Grinder. You can learn how to build rapport with a wide range of stakeholders by matching their body language and tonality, but being genuinely interested in others is just as powerful, if not more. People do have different communication styles and you do need to learn to match them, but sincerity and honesty is everything. Lose someone's trust even over a little thing and it will be difficult to work with them from then on. The art of listening is vital, as everyone wants to get a fair hearing no matter what the situation. It may be tempting to interrupt or focus on getting an immediate decision, but it is quite easy to lose both verbal and non-verbal rapport in these situations. Sincerity is everything, and once you lose trust the business or personal relationship is over.

Always look for referrals from a trusted source and it is important that you build a good network both off and online. These people can vouch for you and a strong network does enhance your personal influence. It is tempting to try and build this too fast or with minimum sincerity. When I had to build new networks within new organisations to create change, no approach works better than giving people some time and doing your best to help them and understand their position.

It is also important to be yourself. I have received a lot of awards and had a lot of impact in my area and sometimes I must share this information in my business building activity. I like to think I do not pretend to be someone I am not and yet in persuading others you are unable to hide your light under a bushel and hope to be discovered. You also must accept rejection when the product or service you are delivering is not what your potential client wants. You are wanting to achieve strategic influence which is long term, and you must walk your talk. Being able to walk away from short-term deals that are lucrative but that could bring long-term problems is vital.

Having the capacity to make a good speech is incredibly important as you can have an opportunity to reach a large audience immediately with future potential business or networks if you inspire them and show you understand their problems.

You will encounter rivals and people who will attempt to damage your credibility for short-term gain. You must deal with this without stooping to the same level and walk away where appropriate. You must not be too sensitive but instead focus on being respectful and focus on long-term opportunities.

Your communication style will depend on who you are dealing with. Always do your homework before a meeting or presentation and always play the numbers game. Every 'no' is part of your learning curve and if you keep responding to feedback you will have your successes. Being linked to organisations with good brands or individuals with an excellent reputation will enhance yours, but it takes time. The key challenge is dealing with the rejections and the opportunities you do not get but which you deserve.

Always research your audience, be they large or small, and learn from both the negative and positive feedback. Never take it personally – learn from the negative and enjoy the positive but keep your feet on the ground. Really care about your audience and the impact you have.

Be flexible – every audience is different – and research key individuals you meet before you have a face to face. Always choose the right style and strategy for each occasion. It is vital to match your communication style to your audience and follow through afterwards on anything you have promised. Everything matters, including how you look, your tonality and how your respond to difficulties and challenges you haven't planned for. Be authentic no matter what and be yourself.

Always be prepared to adapt a little. Your high energy keynote might need adjusting a little, for instance, for an academic audience.

Professor Robert Caldini did a lot of academic research on persuasion, which is the key objective for personal influence. His key findings in his book *Influence: The Psychology of Persuasion* (published by HarperBus in 2007) were that consistency and social proof were important, and building your reputation on a strategic basis. Show yourself to be an authority and build power and social proof. It is lovely to be down to earth and open minded but realise that in personal influence everything matters. Is the phrase 'personal influence' the same as sales? There may be differences but remember you are trying to persuade and do deals to achieve personal and business objectives. Work on your reputation long term rather than short term, inspire but also be seen to be a safe pair of hands and ethical. Quite a challenge, but it can be done. Always remember your personal branding effectiveness can impact on your personal influence.

So, we have reviewed personal influence in a variety of contexts, particularly within organisations of various kinds, but what really is it? Is it really selling yourself, your project or your product in a variety of contexts? My master's thesis subject was on helping car sales staff in a major car company to sell in a professional way through using neuro linguistic programming. Personal influence is about achieving results in a variety of contexts using sales strategies that work within certain defined markets. We should not have to apologise for selling our products, services or time; selling is still sometimes seen as it was represented a few years ago, where it was all about making sales in a very pushy way to vulnerable people.

Personal influence is about communicating persuasively and achieving long-term results. The success and impact you have is very related to your level of personal influence. Have you an audience to communicate with and are you capable of doing it? What impact have you on your audience – do more people buy products or services because of you? No matter what you do in life you need people to offer you jobs, support your business to allow you to participate in decision making. It would be good first to realise that selling is the lifeblood of the economy and that the better you are at it the more you achieve. Your capacity to do it is related to your profile, brand and business and professional networks. Each organisation or area of interest is different but building strategic influence will significantly advance your career or business. How good you are at persuading others and what you do to achieve results depends on the marketplace and your key objectives.

The better you prepare before a pitch and learning from your mistakes will change your results. Inside organisations you can persuade senior management to back projects and achieve rewards and recognition for project success. So, let's look at the skills and mindset of a successful salesperson so you can achieve more sales if you are an entrepreneur or executive or more impact if you work within a company, a university or within the public sector.

A good salesperson believes in the product or service they are promoting. They undertake personal development to build resilience and the capacity to handle unsuccessful pitches. They research the needs of their target group and learn to communicate how their product or service can solve a problem. They can build rapport with their client base and build a strategic relationship. They build an internal and external profile. They prepare well before a meeting and learn from every sales call, successful or otherwise. They realise that sales are a numbers game and know the number of sales calls and face-to-face pitches are needed to achieve a level of success.

So, you can see that personal influence is basically your capacity to reach others and have a positive impact to achieve your own or your company's goals. There are many ways of communication and you will need to develop your process of finding a market and being able to reach it. Many people would be horrified to think they were selling, as the word has

negative connotations of old-style selling where interested
people were not identified but was more a numbers game and
everyone was given the 'hard sell' to eventually selling something. Those days are long gone but if you are trying to get
new business, a project buy in or financial support you have
got to get support from key influencers and agreement to taking the project forward. The most effective type of personal
influence is where strategic relationships are built, and effective communication leads to meeting people's needs inside
and outside the organisation. This is a skill you will want to
develop to enable you to undertake interesting assignments.
Communication is vital for everyone, and we all represent a
company, university or a public body that wants to influence
others either to commit to products or services or to change
as an individual or organisation. All the E Factors are vital but
persuasive communication is the priority needed to achieve
successful projects. Embrace personal influence and use it to
achieve your goals and impact, whatever your background.
Who are you communicating with today and what do you
want to achieve?

Like all the E Factors it is not enough to know that you
should learn this. You must practise and learn from any mistakes. You are trying to develop unconscious competency and
daily habits, you have a role and a job to do or a project to
run. How can you do it and make an impact? Start where you
are now and decide what you want to achieve over the next
six months. Find the communication style that works for you
and your internal or external marketplace. Plan, build rapport and communicate in the most effective way. Build your
personal influence beyond its present level and you increase
chances of corporate survival and build an important skill you
will need in the 21st century.

How You Could Use the E Factors Individually or Mix and Match

Individuals need to learn the best methods of using the E Factors as a practical tool. Having the knowledge is good but, in some ways, pointless if you don't apply it. They must be used either individually or together to achieve practical results. Anyone who has attended university knows that you acquire a lot of knowledge in your chosen degree path but to succeed in the outside world you must be able to make things happen. The E Factor model has identified the eight core competencies of the entrepreneur that are needed to achieve results.

Many people feel they either can only focus on one factor at a time or try to use all eight at once. Neither of these models is the definitive answer as there is no one way to achieve the solution. It is, however, hard as an individual to use all eight at once though much easier if you are working in a team of four or more. However, in many cases applying the most relevant E Factor will produce most of the results. Let me give you an example. You have been asked to produce an idea that will make students more motivated at college. You are searching for a new idea or best approach so the most obvious E-Factor competency to use is creativity, which is using the right side of your brain to create an innovation. You need to focus either individually or as a group in brainstorming as a group and in using the right side of the brain, which many people don't do from age eleven onwards when they leave primary school. You must work to create connections between different things and keep going until you discover an idea with potential.

It is suggested that you run creativity sessions on a regular basis for your group as it requires different thinking to the seven other E-Factor competencies which focus on how to make an idea happen in the real world. Without innovative ideas or innovations organisations will not adapt to the challenges of the 21st century. Creativity requires a different approach because of the need for divergent thinking and yet it is vital, as it is the one skill or area that cannot be potentially replaced by artificial intelligence. It is also suggested that when you or your team are using one of the other seven factors, use creativity to brainstorm ideas and innovations in the competency area being explored. Let's say, for instance, you are developing a personal branding strategy to build the profile of an organisation or individual. You will obviously look at social media and other marketing strategies to boost profile, create awareness and potential market opportunities.

Brainstorming and creating alternative approaches may be one way to broaden a product or individual's appeal.

It is important to consider whether you use one of the E Factors on their own or together to create maximum impact. I have already given you an idea of always using creativity in your use of the other seven E Factors, as using it will create potential innovative ideas and alternative working methods for the other seven E Factors.

Mixing and matching is always possible. It depends on the problem being solved or the opportunity that has appeared. However, in short-term projects you need to find what is the key E Factor that we should focus on now for maximum impact.

However, it is useful to limit the E-Factor use to the skills that will have the maximum impact in achieving the key goal being sought or the problem solved.

In bigger projects it may be advisable to use as many E Factors as possible to achieve results. However, the best advice in the short term is to pick the key factor needed to solve the problem and link with creativity to ensure problems are solved on a whole brain basis. The bottom line is that you must remain flexible. Identify the problem and find as a maximum the core E Factors, usually one or two that can be harnessed to solve the problem and get the result.

The E Factor most relevant to the problem should be used and, in many cases, you will need a creative or innovative approach when there is no clear solution to the problem – always remember that every problem has a solution, and your task is to find the most relevant and impactful E Factor to do this.

Part II

Applying the E Factors

If—

by Rudyard Kipling

If you can keep your head when all about you
Are losing theirs and blaming it on you,
If you can trust yourself when all men doubt you,
But make allowance for their doubting too;
If you can wait and not be tired by waiting,
Or being lied about, don't deal in lies,
Or being hated, don't give way to hating,
And yet don't look too good, nor talk too wise;

If you can dream – and not make dreams your master;
If you can think – and not make thoughts your aim;
If you can meet with Triumph and Disaster

And treat those two imposters just the same;
If you can bear to hear the truth you've spoken
Twisted by knaves to make a trap for fools,
Or watch the things you gave your life to, broken,
And stoop and build 'em up with worn-out tools;

If you can make one heap of all your winnings
And risk it on one turn of pitch-and-toss,
And lose and start again at your beginnings
And never breathe a word about your loss;
If you can force your heart and nerve and sinew.
To serve your turn long after they are gone,
And so, hold on when there is nothing in you
Except the Will which says to them: 'Hold on!'

If you can talk with crowds and keep your virtue
Or walk with Kings – nor lose the common touch,
If neither foes nor loving friends can hurt you,
If all men count with you, but none too much;
If you can fill the unforgiving minute
With sixty seconds' worth of distance run,
Yours is the Earth and everything that's in it,
And – which is more – you'll be a Man, my son!

Chapter 9

Achieving Daily Practice

I am writing Part II to illustrate how to apply the competencies to achieve your goals and help others. Above all, I
want to show you how the E Factor is used in daily life
and how you can put the teachings into practice. The eight E
Factors can be used together or separately in multiple settings,
and I want you to get practical results and maximum benefit.

If you will apply what I teach you it will enhance your life
and your career. Rise to the challenge and enjoy. This is one of
my strategies for helping others and giving something back.

I am using Rudyard Kipling's poem 'If' to illustrate how
the competencies can be used in a variety of situations which
may arise at any time and to show how practical it is and
how the E Factor works. Follow my lead and you have much
to achieve and contribute for yourself and others. Rudyard
Kipling wrote this poem at the time of the First World

War, when he felt his son needed some practical advice and inspiration.

It has inspired me over the years to deal with difficult challenges and provides clear sound advice on how your own behaviour is crucial in challenging times. It does not matter what challenge you face or what opportunity you get, it's all about how you respond that matters. It is up to you! The poem helped me personally at the most important times in my career. At times of great opportunities and of great challenges, allow it to do the same for you.

This is the first line from the poem I want you to discuss: 'If you can keep your head when all about you are losing theirs and blaming it on you.'

This quote resonates with me and is highly relevant in the 21st century where technological change has created constant transformations and challenges for us all. To survive these changes depends on how well we respond and react. When you have a responsibility for a project or a business most people are supportive when things are going well. However, this can all change not only in a major crisis but even when something challenges the status quo.

As it is often said you get to know who your key supporters are, and who will back you, not just on a short-term basis but during any major challenge. In the 21st century the rise of artificial intelligence and the impact from it in any country can be felt because the world is much more interconnected now.

What I have come to understand is that you must work on yourself and use all the E Factors to deal with many different situations. The first E Factor needed is resilience. This is the capacity to stay calm in unexpected or challenging circumstances. You need to develop your capacity to relax and sometimes even detach in unexpected circumstances. This ensures you do not have a 'knee-jerk reaction', reacting too quickly or instinctively. Take the time to seek support and make strategic as well as tactical decisions. It is important to be a team player and yet in the challenging times set an example and use your leadership skills.

Looking after your physical and mental health is incredibly important at these times, as challenges can be quite stressful. As part of your strategic planning, you should have people and resources in place who are ready with support and encouragement for these challenging times. What I found excellent was to have a network of informal mentors in place and keep communication flowing during the good times. These chosen mentors were extremely helpful to me because they were not involved in the day-to-day running of the businesses and the projects, so they always remained detached and objective. To ensure you stay in control, you must be checking in regularly with yourself on your physical and mental health, ensuring you are coping, or identifying when you need help.

Often when I found myself in an incredibly challenging situation, feeling I couldn't see any effective way out, I thought of Rudyard Kipling's words, and they always grounded me and kept me from overreacting. My problems and challenges were resolved much faster because I had worked on my core resilience and was able to use my E-Factor personal influencing skills to inspire and set an example for my team.

Remaining calm and not reacting allows you to think ahead strategically, and to communicate in an empowering way with all stakeholders involved. I also used my creativity E Factor to set up a workshop where my team and I brainstormed all sorts of solutions including some amusing ones and arrived by accident at a solution that sorted out the challenge short term and calmed everyone by having fun and thinking creatively. The key message is not only will you make better decisions if you remain calm, but you will be influencing every other stakeholder inside or outside the organisation to adopt the same attitude!

Keeping your head in short-term crises is something you will learn and can build on.

One of the things I recommend is setting up a community of practice to support each other with internal and external stakeholders. Some people, and particularly entrepreneurs, like to work on their own, and this can be very isolating and detrimental, when it comes to them seeking support, or even advice. Recognise that you live in a constantly changing environment, where there are many others facing similar challenges, and by sharing experiences and knowledge you can all learn and help each other.

You have a strong arsenal of weapons with the E Factor. Practise and use them so you will respond in a positive way when unexpected challenges appear. Resilience, calmness, teamwork, and leadership are all infectious and will help everyone. It is exactly how a good leader should behave. Remaining calm with good team decision-making will enable a problem to be tackled and sorted more effectively. Be your own person and set an example!

Chapter 10

The Power of Dreams

The second highly inspirational extract from the poem 'If' by Rudyard Kipling focused on setting long-term objectives as teams: 'If you can dream – and not make dreams your master.'

This suggests having a vision for the future but backing your vision with action to turn a plan into reality. Many individuals and organisations set out a long-term vision of where they would like to go without building the organisation or team needed to make it happen.

It is great to have a vision and a strategic plan to back it up. Kipling makes it noticeably clear. It is important to think ahead where you want to be one year, five years and ten years ahead and of course to make a practical plan to get there.

Many people have a strong long-term vision and know what they want but do not have the plan to take the tactical steps to get there. The poet knew that too often without a plan or a vision you might have a functioning project, but you stay in the same place or even go backwards if you don't have practical, more short-term business plans to build progress step by step and grow organically.

He was right, and his words are even more relevant nowadays. You can make all sorts of long-term strategic plans but at best you will constantly need to adjust them, particularly when technology is throwing up new opportunities and challenges daily. Kipling had two types of people in mind, and it is amazing how more than one hundred years later the advice is more relevant than ever.

The irony is of course that many people have no long-term career or life plan. Many who have a strategic plan or long-term dream are not taking the practical actions on a daily, monthly or yearly basis that will support their long-term strategy.

With the E Factors you need the visioning long term, and the tactical steps and adjustments to get there. It is rare to find someone running a small business on a day-to-day basis have more than a short-term plan to survive. There are also senior managers in large corporates who know all the long-term trends and have no step-by-step plan to get there. It is difficult to get the balance between strategic thinking and tactics, but you must have it in your own projects. Ideally you should have access to both a strategic and a tactical thinker and use your other E-Factor skills to bring them together for maximum impact. There is no harm in dreaming or visioning but you need clarity and the practical steps and resources to make it happen.

To ensure you achieve your dream or vision, you must use the other E Factors to help to get you there.

Do your research, make your plan, and set out the steps you need to take and a method to review progress. Seek objective, constructive but truthful feedback that identifies problems or behaviours that could endanger the long-term potential of the project.

You rarely find people at the earliest stage of their career who are thinking strategically with a step-to-step implementation plan. They are most likely to be the most successful, but they still require a mix of advisers and contacts to support each other. It is why I am greatly in favour of Communities of Practice, where people support each other in their plan and provide objective feedback on steps taken and opportunities missed.

Kipling was quite right to warn his son not to 'make dreams your master'. His son could dream of what he could do after the war was over but, in the meantime, he had to face everyday challenges and even dangers in the interim. It is rare to find an individual who is focused on daily activity and who also has a strategic five- or ten-year vision. Let's take an example of finance and money. You must get short-term cash flow and have a job or business that enables you to survive and thrive. Equally you need to plan for the long-term, establishing the steps to achieve income for family and retirement plans.

There is no point in having dreams if you will not take the daily steps to move them forward. Find the ways to progress with your long-term goal. With all the E Factors it is so important to use them daily until they become habits that you do automatically. Dare to dream and have a long-term plan. Get mentoring support or at least someone to ask you the difficult questions. If you could find a way to use all the other E Factors both on a short-term basis and in a strategic way you will significantly increase your chances of success,

The right daily habits and action without losing sight of your dream will make it more like an achievable long-term project.

Wise words of advice from Kipling. Too often I see people who act every day and survive, or someone who is always thinking twenty years ahead without doing anything now. Combine the two approaches and you achieve both goals, which should be your key objective.

Entrepreneurs and students find it hard to think long term. Large company and public sector executives will be thinking at least one year ahead but also looking at trends over the next ten years. As I mentioned in the strategy section in Chapter 6, as an accountant at one stage of my career, I focused on my short-term income while trying to help my clients survive daily. I have also worked in large organisations like universities where the five-year strategic plan was everything, with little thought to the daily actions to achieve the objectives. If you think short term, you are susceptible to change. Dream big, dream often and build your E-Factor habits to make the greatest impact short and long term.

My third quote from this famous poem is: 'If you can bear to hear the truth you've spoken twisted by knaves to make a trap for fools, or watch the things you gave your life to, broken, and stoop and build 'em up with worn-out tools.'

Rudyard Kipling also prepares us for the reality that even with our finest ideas we will face opposition, and sometimes projects that we have put our heart and soul into could be destroyed either deliberately or by outside forces. The question is, what can you do in this situation and how will you recover?

Sometimes you make a project a success despite everything and then it gets destroyed by outside forces. In my own career in the university sector, I was brought in to rescue a project that was not working, and I managed to turn it around and implement my E-Factor model to bring about the changes required. The model was a fantastic success and within a couple of years was the number one model in the world. Whilst carrying out this challenging work I was given great support from senior management who were delighted to finally get a working model that met the project's funding requirements, and within four years it became extraordinarily successful and won many national and international awards. Of course, I had worked extremely hard to turn the project around and make it a success, but having the support and backing played a significant role in helping the model be accepted and go on to be successful.

Then suddenly things began to change and quite dramatically, my support system was being depleted as many of the senior management team had retired or left the organisation. They were replaced by others who had no interest in continuing with the project. As far as they were concerned it had achieved its goal and was no longer a priority for the university.

Then the scenario that Kipling had envisaged happened. The project lost its funding, and I lost my staff and the support level plummeted. Eventually I had no choice but to leave. I feel in a one-year period through no fault of my own, all support and interest were withdrawn. Everything I had worked so hard to achieve was lost nearly instantly and I was left feeling quite deflated. After an interim period, I went on to have remarkable success elsewhere but the whole scenario taught me lots of lessons that I remember to this day. I literally had to, as Kipling indicated above, 'watch the things [I] gave [my] life to, broken, and stoop and build 'em up with worn-out tools'.

My confidence was at an all-time low, until I realised I had the answer right in front of me. I began using the E-Factor model to change things around. For several years I had worked for sixteen hours a day. I was exhausted physically and mentally. Now I had to work on my own resilience and as a priority manage my own physical and mental health. I had to learn acceptance, understand that my model had worked but had also been dependent on senior management support. That all changed because of the priorities of new leaders, which can happen in any organisation, and at any time. I needed to use my E Factors to turn things around for me now. I worked on my physical health and got fit but more importantly I accepted what had happened and it taught me a few tough lessons. I was grateful for the opportunity, and I would go on to create a new project in a unique environment, as a much wiser and humbler person. I started off slowly, I did some keynotes and patiently looked for a new opportunity and was incredibly grateful for the support I was beginning to receive.

The truth is I spent three months working in the garage of my house – there was no other space, and 'working from home' had not been tried and tested yet. The garage was cold, though thankfully not damp, and I was surrounded by fitness equipment, garden furniture, and odd bits and pieces. None very conducive for motivating me, or so I thought. I realised I did not want to spend too long working here.

I tried to get a new role and applied for many jobs in universities throughout the UK and Ireland. Most of these were at a much lower level than my previous roles, but I was attempting to rebuild my confidence and self-worth. I felt I had lost my balance. Strangely, I usually got an interview for all the positions I applied for but was never appointed. In the feedback, I was often told I was overqualified for the position.

I was extremely disappointed – rejection is not easy. Of course, I knew I was overqualified, but I was willing to start again. I was rebuilding. By continually applying my E-Factor skills I became more relaxed and confident step by step. Resilience obviously to keep me learning and creativity to develop new projects and a more effective model than before, so that when my opportunity came, I would be ready to implement it when I got the chance. It came four months after I had left my previous post and took up working from the garage.

I was using strategic thinking and was clear what I wanted to achieve when the opportunity eventually appeared. How could I create a more effective project with a greater impact than before that I could walk away and leave. What I was working on was to create a new model where over 200 educators would do the enterprise work themselves and I would lead the community of practice and at any time I knew I could walk away.

Within two years it won the USASBE Outstanding Global Award and eight others, including best in Europe. Opportunities arose and international work including some with China, USA and Europe were commissioned. I was able to walk away after three years, having learnt so much from that experience. I learnt humility, strength, work balance and how to bounce back no matter what happens, no matter what was destroyed. I also accepted that the tough experiences would teach you a lot and once you have been there and learned the lessons you are always ready for the next opportunity, knowing you can succeed.

Most of all I learned how to walk my talk! I learned how fragile I could be and how we can easily become attached or dependent on one outcome or one type of support. Never become too attached to any organisation or project. Think strategically from the start. What do you want to achieve, and do you have an exit plan? Most of us don't because we feel we will not need one if we are successful.

My suggestion to you is to exercise, meditate, and visualise every day. Practise and apply your E-Factor skills at every opportunity. Use the right side of your brain and start your day with some creativity exercises. What is the most outrageous idea that you can produce? Build your own brand. Never totally focus your personal branding on one organisation. Create and re-create if necessary. Have a network of contacts that you can use separately from your present employer or project.

Use various methods of communication to build your personal influence. Handle your financial affairs and build multiple streams of income so that you are not financially dependent on one organisation. Build your physical and mental abilities every day. Become a leader and support others and build focused and empowering communities both inside and outside your present organisation. Get yourself the best deals. Try not to fall in love with an organisation. Using the E-Factor skills will ensure your success particularly if you train yourself and your team to use them.

Accept that with all projects, opportunities and threats are always there. When you are capable relish the challenges and accept the defeats. Learn and get up and keep moving forward. The person who can be humble and resilient and support others is a fitting example of E Factor success. Enjoy the challenges, enjoy the journey.

No matter what you achieve, become a lifelong learner – learning life's lessons not only to improve yourself but also to help others. Sometimes the most impactful lessons come when projects or organisations change, and these challenges will provide you with a wealth of experience and knowledge that you will use again at some time on your journey.

Use the E-Factor model to tackle the next challenge the universe sends you. Going back to basics, after years of success can be tough but with the lessons learned will be more rewarding. It's the way of the world in this era of global technological change. Are you ready to act and help others to do the same?

Chapter 11

Being Yourself

My final lesson from Rudyard Kipling – a poem that has been an inspiration throughout my life:

If you can talk with crowds and keep your virtue,
Or walk with Kings – nor lose the common touch,
If neither foe nor loving friends can hurt you,
If all men count with you, but none too much

I am asking you to learn and apply the eight E-Factor competencies which will make you much more effective and successful, but I am not asking you to change yourself. You may have to modify your behaviour or actions at times but try to always be your own true authentic self. No matter what situation you face, whether it is a big opportunity or a problem.

I have had great successes and some very tough moments both in my career and personal life. Do not be swept along with what appears to be the most popular or contemporary views. Always be yourself, which can at times be challenging, especially if you often feel you do not fit in with the in-crowd, or to be more specific the in-crowd at a certain time. Success and failure can be temporary – they come, they go, some get lost along the way and reappear at another time. You always need to be both strategic and indeed resilient in the good and the not-so-good times. I respect people and I do not judge a book by its cover, and at times this can be difficult, and it takes experience. Don't feel you have to put on an act when developing your E-Factor skills or hide behind them.

Perhaps you are given the opportunity to meet someone who is famous or a top leader in their field. You will be nervous, excited, what a fantastic opportunity – so how will you behave? Try not to sound too clever or boastful of your success. Be honest about who you are and what you have achieved. Or talk about what you're hoping to achieve. Should you get the opportunity, ask for some advice. If that person is not interested with that then move on, you have done enough. However, what you will find is that most successful people are just like you and me and you are much more likely to build rapport with them if you are polite and interested in them. You are not trying to impress or hustle them, you are grateful for the opportunity to meet with them and be part of their environment. One of the people who taught me this was our late Queen of the UK, Queen Elizabeth. I was privileged that it was her majesty who awarded me my OBE for Enterprise Education. As she put the pin onto my lapel, she took a little time to understand what I had achieved and we had a very interesting conversation where she gave me some advice that I have kept confidential, as it was just for me. It showed how excellent Kipling's advice was to learn to be relaxed and yourself especially in the company of important or famous people. They do appreciate it.

On a different level, but equally impressive, was when I met a well-known television sports presenter on the steps of my hotel in Carlisle a few years ago. I recognised him and said hello and without any further ado he started a conversation with me.

What made an impact with me was he kept asking me questions about my work and was genuinely interested in me and what I was hoping to achieve. Very much not our view at times of famous people, or how we think they are going to react with us mere mortals. The E Factor has also been endorsed by one of the presidents of the United States. He turned out to be a great communicator and quite different from his public profile when I met him. Because public figures have a great network of people teaching them how to act and react in public, sometimes this ensures we don't get to meet their authentic self. It's all about using your communication skills, making sure that as well as speaking you are listening and building rapport.

I would love to say in my successful phases during my career that I remained the same old me. I did change or, I believe, success changed me. I became focused with winning international awards, one after the other, and I still craved more. I was being treated as the latest guru who had all the answers, and people sought out my company, and invited me to many major events. I was also delivering many international keynotes in front of exceptionally large audiences. I thought I was being quite laid back and still my humble self until I was taught a lesson. I was in India doing a keynote for five thousand people and received the usual applause and people coming up to shake my hand. Then as I was walking towards the car provided by the Indian government to transport me back to my hotel, a group of young students from the audience rushed over to me and knelt in front of me and they all touched my feet. I was amazed and I thanked them. Now this was heady stuff for me, and with conceit I remarked to the driver of my car, 'I am getting a bit of a rock star status. Did you notice what those students just did?' 'I certainly did,' he replied, 'that was very touching as what they did is a sign of respect for the elderly in India.'

All notions of being like a rockstar evaporated there and then. I was the elderly. It was great that they showed respect for me, and I do believe I became humbler from that moment.

Being yourself and not putting on any airs and graces when things are going well is essential to keep you balanced and grounded. You are a person learning how to develop the twenty-first-century skills for success. Hopefully, you can achieve your goals, but don't allow the ego to take over or treat people differently because of their position, name or achievements. I have never been one of those people who treats someone differently because of their position and it is neither strategic nor effective communication to do so.

As Kipling says, be a good communicator and respect everyone without depending on someone's patronage or having to become a different person because of someone else's position or even perceived success. For me, the most important thing is that someone is respectful of others even if there is no business deal to be achieved. I am sympathetic, it will be something you will have to personally go through. There will always be people who could open doors for you for a price but learn to keep your integrity.

Focus on your own development with your E-Factor skills. Be detached about short-term outcomes and keep learning from successes and failures.

If you can be detached both in the good and the tough times, be resilient and keep moving forward. You are more likely to be successful overall.

Think about what Kipling is suggesting and understand that nothing is certain. It will be hard if an individual or organisation is sending you or your business all their work at the minute. Then they withdraw it. Here you need to find the balance between being too positive or negative. Just be yourself and no matter who you are dealing with, treat everyone with respect. People in a position to give funding or opportunities are wary of people who try to be too clever or insincere. They have the experience to pick this up, and in today's market funders are looking for honesty and sincerity.

The ability to communicate with everyone and people from different perspectives is great, both in your personal life and through business. I do believe in Karma and what you put out there will come back to you. Use the E Factor and you will achieve your goals.

Become a lifelong learner and an honest communicator. Unbelievably your opportunities will come, sometimes a few together, which will test you. If you are communicating in several ways and showing your skills, interest and an intention, you are on the right pathway. When success arrives keep humble and don't change. It is better behaviour and much more strategic. Never care too much for companies' projects or even important contacts – keep focused on the goal ahead. Be yourself, act and learn and you will be a success!

An important aspect is to try and not take yourself too seriously. We can get too caught up in the result and miss some of life's lighter and interesting experiences. Look around you, not just forward. Learning the eight E Factors will help immensely but remember you will always be a work in progress, always looking and finding diverse ways, untrodden paths that you will need to explore. Do not judge others on their position or potential usefulness to you. Getting business and career success is a long-term achievement. Treat others who you meet along the way, as you would like to be treated. Some you will enjoy, others you will wish to avoid – that's life, choose wisely. Try to keep your ego out of everything. Always know that in any situation you face, you can deal with it, and at any time, that you can move on, try again, or try a different approach. Be yourself and understand the potential within you.

Chapter 12

Going Global

I want to show you what the crucial E-Factor skills are if you want to operate on the world stage. This applies to everyone, as the Fourth Industrial Revolution connects the world and we are all affected by innovative technology and by what happens within any one country – actions that reverberate and influence with a global impact, which can't be ignored and must be dealt with.

What do you need to learn and what could you share with others? We are all in a struggle for stability and we all face new threats and opportunities routinely. Sharing and working with others makes us stronger and more creative.

This applies not just to people in the education system but to us all. I have promised you E-Factor skills for 21st-century survival and I have spent many years developing this new model. The original model was extremely successful and way ahead of its time, as most influencing ideas usually are.

Now is the time to give you the skills, mindset and opportunities presented by the new technological world. Health is certainly a factor, both physical and mental. This is why resilience has replaced personal mastery and is now the core skill from which everything emanates.

There is a recognition that you will face constant disruption and challenges wherever you are and whatever you do. You need the physical and mental health to overcome these challenges and turn them to your advantage. You also will begin to understand that you can change circumstances and learn to stay positive in the troubling moments.

You will need digital skills, which was the key skill academics in Liverpool identified as a potential add-on to the E-Factor model. I see them as particularly relevant to personal branding and personal influence, but it is a core skill right across the E Factor as digital tools enhance everything, from finance to learning and creativity.

You will need to find new and unorthodox ways of learning. This will be covered in more detail in the next chapter.

Many recommendations from my initial book have proved to be even more important in the 21st century. How can you learn global skills and how can you take charge of your own learning outside the classroom so as not to hinder your learning beyond the standard institutional curriculum? One pertinent message is that travel can provide all sorts of learning opportunities. This advice came from an ex-student who had become a successful international retail entrepreneur. During a meeting where she was giving the university a large cash donation, she informed everyone to travel as much as possible, as this would enhance their learning opportunities and give them plenty of challenging experiences – a valuable insight over 10 years ago. Take advantage of every travel opportunity you get. Enjoy and keep looking for things to learn, there will be many.

Unfortunately, with Covid-19 came lockdown across the world, and travelling all changed, as different countries scrambled to put into place rigid strategies to control the virus and people travelling through countries. These learning experiences were essential to keep us safe.

Post-pandemic, travel is still often disruptive and challenging but thankfully we can once again travel a lot more freely, and so reap the benefits of the experience.

Try designing your own learning projects whether you are based in an academic institution or working in a large corporate organisation or in the community.

The E-Factor model was seen as rebellious when I originally designed and published it as a curricular model embedded in every degree subject.

They are the key attributes that every person, whether in the education system or not, must attain. To make it happen institutionally, the staff of higher education institutions and their stakeholders must change dramatically, and until they do you must in the interim take charge of your own learning. If you are currently still at an institution, make sure you get a valuable experience that genuinely prepares you for the 21st century.

What can you learn from your recent or present institution? Can you take the initiative, do you have the skills, or just the grades? Are you now completing graduate or professional education? The reality is every situation will vary and you must ultimately take charge of your own education, training and skills plan.

Maybe you feel this does not seem fair if you or your funder have significant fees to pay. You cannot grow and develop in the global economy if you don't take charge of your education. What action are you going to take? Apply the E-Factor model to help you in all areas. Always continue searching to enhance your creativity.

The E-Factor competencies are so important because whatever stage you are at now and whatever you have attained educationally the E-Factor skill model, which I originally designed from my work with entrepreneurs, is relevant for everyone as the educational and learning landscape begins to change. The model was originally designed for students of any subject area who either wanted to start their own business or explore innovation. Now and for the near future it's become so much more relevant to everyone. Traditionally it was mainly art and creative students who had to look at a portfolio of roles. Now it's everyone.

The Fourth Industrial Revolution can be defined as 'a fusion of overwhelming technological breakthroughs coming almost simultaneously'. There are so many mega trends, and we will all need to find the right answers to sustain ourselves. Think global in everything you do. I am sure your education provider or employer are thinking this way and hopefully through my continuous requests you are getting the message. We all need to be entrepreneurs now. We all face uncertainty and need to take charge. Exciting and bewildering, I know, but what an opportunity. Go for it!

Part III

E Factor Application

Chapter 13

Using the E Factor

Reading a book is the first stage. Applying it is next. I don't want to undermine the value of your educational or work experience to date, I just want you to be ahead of the game and turn the Fourth Industrial Revolution into an opportunity. All I can do is give you the warnings, the opportunities and the answers. You must use them. Some of you will and you will thrive. Some of you will take a half-hearted approach. A few of you will do well. As for the rest of you, all I can do is remind you that you know what you must do. Find a way to make it happen. I will give you lots of suggestions, tools and strategies. It's up to you.

So, let's look at some of the things you can do. I have made a lifetime of study of entrepreneurship and personal development. I am not saying it is easy for any of us to apply them.

I have seen a few people who have become millionaires or high-impact change agents. Which do you want to be?

So, let's apply the E Factor to this global trend.

What lies ahead? Have you done some strategic thinking and applying?

How have you prepared your mental and physical armour, commonly known as resilience? How are you taking charge of your learning? Prepare for the challenges ahead of time then you will be ready. What I really want you to do is to take charge of your E-Factor learning. You can attend a course and implement some of the habits but it is down to you. It's your responsibility. Contact me anytime and I will show you a direction to go in.

I can't highlight enough that you need practical and academic learning. I love knowledge and learning things but for me it is the ultimate failure if you have the knowledge that shows you want to succeed but none of the learning skills and motivation to make it happen. Please listen to me – I speak from the heart and with much knowledge and experience.

What is your style of learning that works for you? Take charge of it, it's up to you whether you are on a course or not. Time is of the essence, do something now.

Once you know what you should do, get out and practise it. There is no other way, you know what to do and can tell everyone else, but if you don't practise it regularly yourself, you will lose all benefits. You need someone to report to and you might put a little positive pressure on yourself. I am always contacting my mentors and supporters to challenge me and keep me grounded. Find your mentor guide or friend who is prepared to do the same for you.

Intention

Set your intention – what are you aiming to do? What are your priorities in making a successful transition in the Fourth Industrial Revolution? When you manage it, how can you help others? You need to plan your own agenda and use the E Factors together.

Ask yourself the E Factor questions:

1. What do I want to create and where do I want to make a difference?
2. What will I do step by step?
3. What target will satisfy me?
4. Can branding and influence help?
5. What resources do I need?
6. Who will I report to?
7. When will I exit to the next project?
8. Who mentors me?

You may think you know all the answers, but you need accountability and to learn from every experience.

Chapter 14

Working with Global Technology

We need to embrace the advantages of working with global technology and plan to deal with the likely challenges.

We certainly need to embrace artificial intelligence (AI). Ask yourself the question: how can it help us and how can we deal with any potential areas of negativity? It is neither good nor bad and it is how we can use it for the greatest impact. You can use it to perform routine tasks, but what industries does it threaten? The biggest challenge is dealing with the extreme views towards it. Some people will see it as either an advantage or disadvantage. It can't replace some of the E-Factor skills such as creativity. We must learn to live with technology, learn all about and use it where appropriate, without thinking it is a panacea for all ills.

We need to think critically and use it to the best advantage. The reality is that AI can process a lot of data but creativity for the individual is an even more prized skill. Ultimately, handled right it will only enhance our processes and offer greater opportunity to focus on creative thought and impact.

Use the E Factor to get out of your comfort zone. It offers an opportunity to focus on skills and personal development models such as the E-Factor model. Less time will be taken up on doing logical tasks. I genuinely believe with the E Factor it can be a win–win task.

With the E Factor, globally people can focus on creativity risk and teamwork and eliminate routine tasks – this can only be a good thing.

The E Factors are the real skills to make people both more successful and employable. We can all focus more of our time on skills and mindset and less on routine administration work.

In applying the E Factor we must focus on global competence. We need to be creative to find links between different international groups. We all need to embrace the new economy and build connections and trust. The Fourth Industrial Revolution gives us an opportunity to change work and the education system and focus on personal development and competencies rather than on traditional analysis and logical mindsets. This is a serious opportunity to create global competence creativity and a strong well-linked global community of excellence on a massive scale.

The E Factor originally evolved to meet the challenge that an ex-prime minister set the education and skills system. He hoped to create more technological entrepreneurs, but he was convinced that students of all disciplines would benefit from learning how to be creative and innovative because of the global link-up that technological development would bring. There is still much work to be done to achieve this, partly because university and college systems were not geared to skills and development but to knowledge and analysis. In spite of the creation of A1 this is still very much the case over twenty years later. You need to take personal responsibility for your own development as academic research requirements and professional education still do not place enough evidence on soft skills and creativity. This is likely to change but not for the foreseeable future.

As a potential or actual E-Factor practitioner you have a terrific opportunity to apply these skills as traditional educational models break down to accommodate the new emphasis. This will take time to happen for the next generation. If you are eighteen and over, I urge you to embrace these E-Factor skills, inside or outside the curriculum.

You need to embrace them to develop global skills and opportunities, which was the reason the shortfall was identified in 2000.

You can create massive impact and help others to achieve their potential but only by working within the present system and applying the eight E-Factor competencies to help others do the same, either by being an example or by coaching them. Go for it!

Chapter 15

E-Factor Learning

I am happy that you have either bought or been given a copy of this book. I hope you find it useful and enjoyable. It is my life's work, and I am honoured to share it with you. However, it is all a waste of time if you don't make it part of your life, build the competencies, apply them in your work and personal life and share them with others.

This may seem a little strong, but brutal honesty is crucial at this stage. I feel myself and others have developed models which will help anyone face the challenges and opportunities that the global economy brings if they will apply and use them on a regular basis. To make skills unconscious and part of your daily behaviour, requires using and applying them regularly until they become as a normal routine without thinking.

I had a conventional education like many other people. A levels, degrees and postgraduate qualifications, with a lot of the focus on completing academic assignments. I am not saying this is not a good education, but it is not enough. Your entire future depends on you making things happen and turning change into opportunity in the global economy. To do this you need a range of unconscious competencies that will enable you to cope with change, develop creative ideas and make them happen. Otherwise, you tend to behave in a way based on your experiences.

So, what should you do about it? Well either by good judgement or good luck you are reading the book to help you make things happen but unless you apply your learnings it will all have essentially been a waste of time. Maybe you will tell someone else about the E Factor and they will apply and achieve the results you were aiming for. In your own way you have contributed by sharing the model but by not using it you have missed an opportunity. In this section of the book, I will share the methodology that works. The next stage will be to use it to help yourself and others. Enjoy the rest of the book but I have issued my warning. So do not miss the opportunity.

The first thing you must do is complete a self-assessment on your level of competency in the eight core E Factors. The test is very rigorous and was designed by an eminent Scottish psychologist.

I also suggest that you get a third party to complete a questionnaire on your behalf to provide a second independent opinion. Are you competent in them? What are your strengths and weaknesses? How are you going to improve the weak scores or harness the strengths you clearly have? It does not matter where you are now, but I hope you will build competency and get support. Or in some cases, you use your strengths and abilities to make a difference for yourself and others.

I suggest as well as completing the questionnaire monthly you keep a daily journal. Record any use of the competencies, what happened and what are your learnings. It is part of the method of you using some or all the competencies on a daily basis, holding yourself accountable and continuing to work on your improvement daily. You may miss days and it could take a while for it to become a habit, but it is well worth it. If you can manage this you will notice the E Factors becoming part of your daily behaviour until they become automatic. It will require self-discipline and patience but if you manage it the E Factor will become part of your skill set and you will be more successful, whatever your job, occupation or business project.

Completing the questionnaire should give you most of the evidence of your performance but an independent review will provide you with another perspective on what you are doing and identify additional training and development if needed. It may show you are not as self-aware as you thought but this will help you get things right and be more effective. There is no doubt you will be honest in completing the questionnaire, but we do need some additional insights to confirm we are on the right track and not stalling or hesitating. Doing the right things daily and getting outside help increases your chances of being more effective on a long-term basis. This all sounds easy, but most people don't do it on a regular basis. As I keep repeating, do everything 100 per cent or accept the consequences.

The Method

You may have a particular style of learning that suits you, but it is important to regularly seek an outside opinion. Practise, for instance, your creativity at least once a day. Thinking divergently sometimes produces what appears to look like an absurd solution to a problem. You will be amazed at times by how innovative solutions come from bringing together a wide range of ideas that seem disconnected. The important thing with the competencies is to use a minimum of four of them together every day so you get used to not using them in isolation. The most powerful solutions will come from using a few of them together. Let's say you need creative thinking to come up with a new solution. You also need to think how you will finance it and how you will use your personal branding to get people interested. You will have a preferred method of operating. Some people prefer face-to-face lectures and some find online or independent learning more appropriate. What works for you? Get some independent opinions, as the learning style that you prefer may not be the right one for you to help develop the skills.

Daily Activity

What you do daily will determine whether the E Factors become something you use to produce results or something you turn to every so often, when you face a difficult situation. We say we are all busy and it is hard to fit much extra in but prioritise your needs. So, keep it simple but continuous. In an ideal world fifteen minutes in the morning and ten minutes at the end of the day to reflect on what you did and to learn from it. This could be highly effective.

It does not seem much but will help you to become a highly effective E-Factor practitioner if you follow this model an average of five days a week for fifteen minutes. Anything more is unrealistic and could be hard to guarantee completion on a regular basis.

What Is Your Learning Style?

We all have a preferred style. It could be learning through action. It could be through reading or through listening to a podcast, for instance. However, gaining knowledge on the areas concerned is not enough if we are aiming at changing behaviour on a lasting basis. Pick an effective method, get help if needed and work on it. Your persistence is especially important to make it a habit. It is challenging to adopt a more active learning process, but the world is full of people with profound knowledge that either won't or can't apply it. Now is the time you can do things differently and effectively. Learning the model is futile if you don't use it on a practical basis, not only to help yourself but also others.

Build Flexibility

Build flexibility into your projects. When trying to solve a problem brainstorm a few different solutions. Don't always tackle a problem with the same process and activities. Use different E Factors in combination or on their own as a solution until you find the right E Factor combination for the right activity. You need to be relaxed in your mindset and enjoy the challenges, where you use some or one of your skills to solve the problems. You will have some strong competencies that make an impact but be aware that every problem to be sorted on a sustainable basis needs a customised solution. The permutations and the mix of skills will open up many opportunities.

Learning Methodology

You need to adopt your own learning methodology, but I recommend the above suggested model that is suitable for people acquiring global skills and adapt it to your particular needs.

Observe what you are learning and the strategies you need. Then use your own learning process that has worked for you to date. You have got the understanding now, but you need to practise and do effective work in applying the E Factor, for instance in a live situation. Once you have applied all these strategies and reflected, find an audience to teach it to – you will find your learning increases and it gives you a different perspective. It's highly effective. I am not trying to turn you into a teacher – I am giving you the most effective learning strategy model. Personally, I learnt creativity through teaching it to students from a variety of backgrounds, including nursing, engineering and science.

Link the E Factors together when you need to. In some cases, use an E Factor such as personal influence, alongside creativity. Use two or three of the eight factors at once and then mix or match them – you will find that they work much better together than separately.

Creativity

Learning creativity and how to teach it is important, as curiosity and innovation are vital in many challenging situations. Creativity and curiosity are core 21st-century skills.

Creativity is the most neglected skill but possibly the most important. Some combination of the other E Factors is always needed alongside creativity to apply it, otherwise you have just produced an idea but not a live project.

A Morning Routine

Try first thing in the morning to visualise your day. Start with the intention of having a good productive day and ask for inspiration to start your day with some innovative ideas. Try to wake up and rise at the same time each morning and work on your physical and mental health. Try and visualise how you want your day to go. In the evening, again around the same time, finish off your day with a review of what you have learnt or experienced, and what you may have done differently. Then take 10 minutes to plan your strategies for the next day. The power of habits will become clear. Establish the routine and watch your impact flourish!

Purpose

Are you clear what you want to achieve not only for the next day but overall?

You have an opportunity to make whatever impact you want if you are true to your purpose. Always come back at the end of the day to your strategic aims and visualise them coming through. Then apply the rest of the E-Factor skills every day to learn as much as possible.

Learning Group

Set up your own learning group and unlock the power of diversity. You will all support each other, learn from each other, and will boost your impact with the power of the learning group. It also pays to be adaptable.

Share Your Story

Speak to diverse audiences throughout the world and you will start to learn on a global basis and get to understand international differences and similarities. It is possible to do some online as well as face to face, which opens the world for you without constant travel. Your own story is more important – it does not matter if it is still short and, in its infancy, you can talk about your aspirations and working with the E-Factor model, what you find working for you and what you are struggling with. One of your aims is to become an E-Factor expert. This provides much learning for your target audience.

Do things your own way. There is no right or wrong and your audience will soon let you know what resonates with them and what else they want to hear from you. The opportunity is there for you to create your own model and your own audiences. I want as many as possible to learn the E Factor and then begin to use it by teaching and helping others.

Create Your Own Community

I will be setting up a global E-Factor community of practice that you will be invited to participate in. I also welcome those who set up their own learner practitioner groups. Learner practitioner groups are communities of practice who meet face to face or online to offer support. The most important thing is to help as many people as possible to achieve for themselves and work with their business, employer, country or region. It's a truly global world now.

Use the technology you are familiar with to reach out. It's good to do some face to face but sustainability pushes us to control our travel. I am writing this in my office in Ireland looking at the famous mountains of Mourne but this book and the E Factor is going international.

Use technology more and you can have greater impact. Embrace technology and yet realise you have a vital role in first building your own skills and then sharing them with others. Test yourself for global competence. You need this and to think from a global perspective on anything local, national and international that happens. I want you to be a global E-Factor expert with an international audience whilst still focusing on living and achieving impact in your own region.

Do not be too focused on classrooms or a required local curriculum but on global E-Factor competence and impact. Do not be a conventional teacher. You can see the global E-Factor skills are needed by everyone everywhere.

Never let formal education interfere with learning and bring creativity and innovation to anything you do. Part of your role is to help people embrace the massive changes and opportunities that are created by technology. Adopt the mindset of Albert Einstein: 'I never teach my students. I aspire truly to provide the conditions whereby they learn.'

The key point is how you will move forward, what you want to do and who can help you. Whatever your role as a teacher, learner or practitioner, what do you want to do? Will you embrace the revolution?

Can you make people be more effective and still be an advocate for globalisation and technological change? Whatever your views you must embrace the new world with excitement knowing that you have a vital role and your opportunity to make an impact is massive. Build a talented team formally or informally. You are a pioneer, and you have an opportunity and a duty to play a role in the world today. Let's get started one step at a time.

You are an E-Factor learner. You are at the start of your journey, but you have an unbelievable opportunity to make a significant impact on your own life, your local community and the rest of the world. The E Factor has been developed and applied over many years and you must use it. It would be unfortunate to come across a model like this at the right time and not use it for your own benefit and that of others. Begin to think first how you will learn this, not just by reading the book but making it part of your skill set. You can't help others until you help yourself first. Once you have done that come back to me and tell me what you want to achieve, however personal, local, or international. I will show you how you can be an E-Factor learner but also what opportunities are open to you. You must be a lifelong learner – or aspire to be – to achieve your goals and you need to help others to do the same. It does not matter how small or large your aspirations are. Help one person or thousands or just focus on yourself or your own family. Being a lifelong learner and practitioner is great for any of us but there is much more to be done – do you want to contribute?

Whatever you want to do or contribute I can show you how to do it. You will find my contact details at the back of this book.

Chapter 16

Coaching and Mentoring Support

Y̶ou can learn the E-Factor model on your own if you are prepared to be self-disciplined, be active, keep journals and reflect daily on your performance. However, you will require mentoring and coaching support to increase your chances of developing and maintaining the competencies. It is hard to be your own mentor and self-coach and it is fair to say we need someone to support us but also to challenge us with straightforward honesty. It will enhance your learning and challenge you. You can do a lot of your E-Factor work yourself, but you do need someone to ask you the challenging questions, someone who is not involved in your day-to-day activity or is part of your family. Do you understand your own needs? If you want to be a high achiever, I do believe this process will enhance your chances of success. Mostly what I wish for you personally is that you are motivated for change and love what you do. You will need to work effectively and keep your thirst for learning and find the right mentor for yourself. Do not accept them because they are the only person available, at this time. Do a trial run and focus on rapport and trust. Reputation and the personal success of the coach or mentor seem the obvious qualities, but it's trust and a real commitment from them to push you to enhance your capabilities and hold you to account. It's a special relationship that will enhance your E-Factor capability. It is also important that they are certified in the model. If you can find someone from your community of practice this will be excellent.

The aim is to help you achieve your potential and be a thought leader in your own field. Find your main coach but you might find a few others who will push you as a member of your community of practice and encourage you to do the same for them. You require the mentoring to become the best version of yourself. Keep true to yourself, you do not need to act or copy another person you admire or aspire to be like. Be your unique self.

I will ask you some coaching questions here to guide you in the E-Factor principles, but I am not your coach. The right one will enhance your capability, your global skills and your impact.

Be humble, even if things are going very well. When you get a chance to mentor someone else formally, accept this and you will understand what a mentor tries to achieve and what their perspective and aim is. The coach or mentor will ask the tough questions that are needed so it is good to get both perspectives on the process. Your mentor does not need to be a person who has a prominent level of achievement. They need to be a good listener and someone you can build good rapport and respect with.

Can you accept that you will have setbacks? We always have setbacks on our road to success. Work on your attitude and set goals with your coach to review on a regular basis. Focus on one goal at a time.

It can be useful to get feedback from a diverse group so decide on the overall best option for yourself.

You need to be self-motivated but need encouragement when you are struggling to change. Some of the best mentors I have had have not been global experts but simply someone who listened and let me arrive at my own solutions. You could also create a small community of practice where you meet and listen non-judgementally to each other. The right type of mentor allows you to talk and simply encourages you and asks a few questions which might guide you in the right direction. It is also important that they believe in you. We all have crises of confidence sometimes and the right person, by genuinely listening, can help with a simple suggestion. It is good to get a second opinion and it is good to get encouragement.

A coach who wants to change everything you do is not the right coach for you. They may think they know best but stay true to your own goals and aims. We all feel better when we are not being judged and we are allowed to get on with things. One of my best mentors was a colleague who did not say much, just listened to me and gave me some advice and practical help in a subtle, non-assuming way. He had no ego himself, he was a great sounding board in times of change. I knew I was never being judged but knew I had his support where possible. I received many accolades and awards, but he played an especially significant role as a sounding board who gave practical help where needed. What was encouraging when I was involved in new developing projects was having someone who listened, was detached, never offered an opinion, and gave help when asked.

Our working relationship finished a few years ago, and when I bumped into him in Belfast recently, I tried to thank him because over the years I realised how much he had helped me with his subtle mentoring and coaching. He refused to take any of the credit. If we all had a mentor like him, we could change the world.

We all require these types of mentors to help us bring about change. This was clear to me even in an organisation where I had massive success but no mentor or anyone who encouraged me throughout the entire organisation. I eventually left for this reason. By using the E-Factor skills when working with people you need to listen, encourage and not judge. Subtly done, this is a powerful tool.

Eventually you will have your own chance to mentor and coach others. You want to inspire them, listen and understand their position, and encourage them. Certain distinctive styles of mentoring suit different people. As I have mentioned earlier in a different context, I once received honest feedback from an ex-colleague who was reviewing my application to become the first UK National Teaching Fellow in Entrepreneurship. When I reacted rather badly to the rejection of my first attempt to draft my submission, she showed great clarity and total honesty: 'Don't bother submitting the proposal again if you are not going to give it 100 percent.'

I was disappointed and hurt but after reflection I knew she was right. I resubmitted a much more professional effort which won the first National Teaching Fellowship and led to multiple successes and opportunities. I never thanked her, which I deeply regret because that was the perfect mentoring in that situation.

You need to know what mix of mentors you need, and you have got to work together as a team. There is no right way to coach or mentor or to be mentored. It depends on the case and the challenge. Find people who know you and encourage you and are prepared to tell you the reality. Learn the lessons. Find your coaching and mentoring team, work together and create impact and global change in the 21st century.

Chapter 17

The History of the E Factor, 2005–2024

There is rather an interesting history around the E Factor. Where did it come from? Did it have any impact? Were there any challenges and where are we now?

Plenty of questions – so let's get it updated and outline our future. It's been quite a journey so far and the mission continues. I have always been interested in achieving goals and was extremely competitive both in the classroom and the sports field but with an average level of talent. I was always open to learning strategies to win and was interested in the mental side of sport. Unfortunately, I was not always particularly good at implementing the strategies. I learned so much myself from teaching youth training students the skills needed to get a job and keep it. I also passed my Chartered Accountancy exams in record time, not through financial talent but because I discovered and implemented the right habits to pass challenging professional exams. I sold my business and became a full-time training consultant at the University of Ulster, providing personal and professional development to female entrepreneurs, public sector executives and company directors. I thoroughly enjoyed this phase of my life. I moved forward in my career to take up a post at a research-based university which had a challenging project. The university had not been successful in getting students of all disciplines to learn how to be innovative and entrepreneurial three years into a four-year project.

I had to engineer a method in which the university staff accepted entrepreneurship and would encourage students to develop the skills of the entrepreneur, while understanding and finding it relevant, whether they wanted to start a business or work as a professional. I developed a model which showed them how to be creative and make an idea happen. The students loved it and enjoyed learning. They began using my skills model to develop new ideas, to start businesses and create social enterprises. It was called the E Factor and was based on many years of advising entrepreneurs and businesspeople who deal with constant uncertainty and change, in the way we all do now. Then I designed a course where students embraced their creativity and the skills to make things happen. The course was a massive success, with over ten thousand students completing this annually. Gordon Brown, the then UK prime minister, had already identified the potential impact of technology on graduates. The government funded over thirty UK universities to teach graduates innovation skills to prepare them for the new global economy. Technology could allow some events that were happening in one country to impact on another.

I had a rigorous questionnaire developed by an occupational psychologist. Every student in every discipline at my university undertook this before and after their course. I then followed this up over a ten-year period. I published several academic papers which showed that over 87 per cent of the students retained and improved their E-Factor skills over a ten-year period and had achieved either excellent career progression or started their own business. The model went international, and I trained over fifty staff sponsored by the European Economic Community (now the European Union) from thirty countries on this model. I also shared my model with several universities in China and India through keynotes and with government officials. This model won forty-five awards over a ten-year period for Queens University Belfast and Liverpool John Moores University.

In Liverpool I created an E-Factor community of practice with over five hundred education staff who used it to help students progress their career.

The first E Factor book was published in 2005. I was fortunate enough to be selected in 2011 as the most innovative educator in the UK by both the Higher Education Academy and by the Times Higher Education Body. My E-Factor programme was voted the best entrepreneurial education programme in Europe in 2016 and the best in the world in 2017 by the United States Association for Small Business and Entrepreneurship.

Since 2019 there have been a variety of E-Factor programmes in the Cumbria region in the UK. Successful pilots have been run with students, executives, apprenticeships and college educators. The E-Factor programme has also been run by a small-business expert in South Africa called Brennan Williams, to address rural poverty, helping over three thousand people create sustainable businesses without any funding. It has also been used to help with regional development and with government officials in Cumbria. Digital E-Factor materials are being developed to make it accessible online and worldwide.

So, although the model has already had a significant impact in a few areas and internationally, there is a recognition at this stage that the model will be used on an international basis to deal with the challenges that the Fourth Industrial Revolution brings. In many ways they are the skills needed by anyone living and operating anywhere in the world. It is all about learning to be sustainable and responding to both the threats and the opportunities that artificial intelligence brings on a global basis. The model will enable anyone to cope with change, make an impact and help others. It is a considerable time of change and this needs to be addressed and solutions adopted and implemented.

Ongoing training is required, and it is necessary to develop mentors who will support students and adults through the change process. It is essential for people who are preparing for new jobs or those who are facing a change in their whole relationship with work. Perhaps the core function of the E-Factor model will help present and future employees to adapt and cope with change and to have positive impact. The E-Factor model has always been aimed at helping people change and innovate but arguably the core skills now need to be learned by everyone to a level of acceptable competency. We all need to learn to be global.

Resilience, creativity, strategic thinking, and communication skills will all be tested on a regular basis, and these are key E Factors for everyone now. Originally it was quite a challenge for people to accept that they needed new skills, particularly as most education prioritised knowledge and understanding and the idea of learning skills was mainly focused on vocational technical education. Soft skills were only seen as relevant for individuals who were embracing them as part of their decision to improve personal development just as an interest. Traditional educationalists would not have been in favour of it being in the mainstream educational curriculum. Now everyone needs a model and practical training and education in personal and management development. This is not a self-improvement journey chosen for a few but a core development plan for everyone who wants to survive and operate in the new economy.

The E-Factor eight competency system is truly relevant as it is the most fitting competency model for 21st-century skills. It will have to ensure that there will be a stronger emphasis on thinking globally. There will be an ever-greater emphasis on taking charge of your own education and taking personal responsibility for your growth and development.

We will need mentors to challenge us. The E-Factor model will challenge you to investigate areas outside your core specialist area. We will need to train many more E-Factor trainers and educationalists and create online programmes to scale up the training. We will need digital versions of the programme to set the need and create a new international online community of practice so we can help each other.

We must encourage people to decide their own curriculum and give them in many cases blended learning experiences customised to their needs.

The education system is changing and the E Factor is in a strong place to make a major international contribution.

Chapter 18

How Can You Become an E-Factor Peak Performer?

To become a peak performer using the E Factor, you will need to develop and adopt a number of habits, outlined below:

1. Love learning from all diverse sources. You do not just decide to become an excellent E-Factor practitioner, you need to adopt the right attitudes and make it part of your daily practice and part of your normal behaviour. Embrace learning no matter what or where it comes from. The world is changing at a rapid rate, and you must enjoy it. Learning can come from all sorts of random activities. What guarantees its success is your attitude to new,

unexpected and sometimes challenging things. Welcome them and be hungry for new learning opportunities no matter where they come from.

2. Take charge of your own learning and constantly search for formal and informal opportunities. Ultimately your destiny, happiness and career trajectory are all down to you. Do something every day and become one of the few who walk their talk and are prepared to learn from everything and share their findings with others.

3. Do not fear failure. You will get all sorts of challenges. Things will not always work out but remember that sometimes the mistakes you make can have the biggest possible impact on your growth and future impact.

4. Yes, embrace learning opportunities but you will sometimes have to know when you need to exit a business relationship and when to stay involved.

5. Mentor others less fortunate than yourself. It is particularly useful being a temporary adviser, but this type of work gives you a new perspective.

6. Do what you love, as this will encourage your motivation. What help can you give others?

7. Deal with rejection and accept the outcome. Rejection is not personal. Keep relaxed, help others and you will find many opportunities.

8. Build your network. Who you know is as important as what you know. Use social media and any face-to-face opportunities to build agreement and collaboration.

9. We all need a mentoring relationship that works for us. Your mentor should be someone external whose views you share on most things.

10. Find your people, challenge them, and engage with them.

11. Give everyone at least one chance to share E-Factor strategies. Be prepared to ask for help. You may be an expert, but you need collaborations to get the biggest impact.

12. Persevere. At difficult times remain resilient. Don't expect immediate impact – your time will come.

13. Make sure you have a genuine passion to learn and help others to build their potential. Learning can come from your greatest difficulties or from mistakes you admit to or from the most unlikely of circumstances. It's the universe conspiring to see whether you are ready to embrace and learn from short-term challenges to create long-term personal growth for you and your team. Enjoy the journey no matter what and both the learning and the impact will come at the right time.

14. Make sure you have a thirst for learning and set an example for colleagues, mentees, or other stakeholders. What they all will be asking is: 'Is this leader consistent with their actions, do they follow this up with their words, do they genuinely want to help me and form a community of learning?'

Follow these guidelines and you can become an E-Factor peak performer. So many people are looking for someone who walks their talk, not just in the good times but in the challenging times also. Life will throw you some tough challenges when you set yourself up as an expert to help others. This is when you must hold firm and be resilient in whatever challenges you face. Be inspired and hold steady. A lot of people are looking to you for inspiration. Act the part of the winner and you will become that person.

Chapter 19

Twenty-One
Steps for Success
with the E Factor

I want to give you some advice on how you can achieve your goals with the E Factor.

It works and many people have already had remarkable success with the updated model. Particularly in the early days I shared this model with everyone but was more concerned with doing this rather than using it every day and turning the model into skills and unconscious competencies. The model is only of practical use if you apply it and mix and match the competencies to achieve your objectives and to make things happen in your field of endeavour. Apply these twenty-one tips and you will make the E Factor part of your work and private life and see the results.

You are reading this book as we head into the Fourth Industrial Revolution and the need to deal with technological change and potential global challenges has never been greater. The most obvious tip is 'use it or lose it'. It's nice to know what having entrepreneurial and innovation competencies can do for you but even better to make it happen and be a live example for everyone else. It is up to you. So here are the twenty-one tips:

1. Have a daily routine for practising and applying the competencies. Make it simple and make it realistic. Keep yourself accountable and find someone who you can report to on a weekly basis. At the end of the day, review your strategy and plan for the day.

2. Find a straightforward way of operating. In this technological age you can use your phone to send short updates to an interested colleague and if it helps, do the same for someone else on the same path.

3. Read relevant material for at least ten minutes every day. Preferably you should be working on some competency you are focused on or some project you are planning to implement.

4. Find a way of helping someone else to apply the E Factor in their life or work. Do it on a voluntary basis. Allocating even an hour a week for this can make a difference and will promote a better E-Factor practitioner.

5. Set up your own community of practice. Have a small but diverse group of people from different areas who are interested in or are also using the E Factor for a different purpose. You will learn so much from each other and

support one another where needed. Your group can meet face to face or online.

6. Set your own strategic and tactical objectives. Put them in writing and write a short but honest feedback report on what you have done and not done.

7. Find a way of spending a little time with Generation Z. These are young people who are trying to cope with the changes that technology enforced. It is important to understand them and allow them to contribute, as they will form a larger part of your future marketplace and need the E Factor more than anyone.

8. Target the audience you care most about. Whatever your own ambitions business-wise or community-based, get started in the market you care about and want to make your greatest impact.

9. Meet with a range of stakeholders once a month.

10. Have clarity on your targeted area and use it to learn, and gain experience. You must use all the competencies individually and together – they all matter. Repeat as required.

11. Keep taking courses yourself. You might understand the model and be helping others with it. No matter who you are or your success to date you need to be a lifelong learner for maximum impact but you are also setting milestones for personal accomplishment.

12. Take one day a week and use one of the competencies in all your activities. You will learn all sorts of ways to use it.

13. Keep up to date with the Fourth Industrial Revolution. It will impact in all you do. Be interested in the details of the innovative technologies.

14. Practise continuous personal development every year. Update, apply and use continually to get the benefits and achieve your objectives.

15. Reach out on any issue. You bought the book so now you are part of the E-Factor family. I want you to enhance your life and make a difference. I have a global community of practice that I want you to be involved in. It's up to you. It's great to buy the book and I genuinely hope that not only have you enjoyed it, but you are using it to achieve something you want to do or help others.

16. Get involved in E-Factor programmes or get certified and design your own. Take your time – the real benefit of the book is to use it and work with others.

17. Use the E Factor to do a random act of kindness a day. What might you do? Use your creativity, resilience and personal influence skills to help people. This is all part of you being a success.

18. You have your own story. What do you want to share with people? Use the E-Factor model to make it happen.

19. Specialise in one of the eight factors first before you learn the others – which one would make the most difference for you or others? Use it in every way possible.

20. Always be relaxed and positive. Appreciate your life and be happy. Enjoy and have fun with the E Factor.

21. Be generous and share.

Chapter 20

Who Needs the E Factor and How Can It Help Them?

The E-Factor model after being used to train university students of all disciplines in Belfast and Liverpool has been used with key stakeholders in Cumbria, including educators, enterprise officers, company executives and civil servants.

It helped the above stakeholders to deal with disruptive change and create sustainable solutions within their own working environment. The E Factor provides generic innovation solutions and there is a need for a specific solution within each niche. It is great that the model can help so many people, but each niche is different, and their specific needs must be addressed. The core eight E-Factor competencies apply to every niche mentioned and to many other areas of training.

Coaching helps make each solution customised and relevant to the targeted niche. The E Factor will help every niche member to be creative, resilient and strategic and to create leadership, communication and marketing solutions – provided all training and coaching is designed for the targeted niche and the solutions it requires. To make it happen in the medium term they need coaches and facilitators from an industry like the course participants.

Small Business Owners

Entrepreneurs and self-employed people are used to dealing with uncertainty but like all participant groups they need training and support to develop all eight competencies in a suitable way to operate in that work area. Small business owners will tend to only have experience in some of the competencies and may need to learn to apply several of the E Factors they are not currently using. Small business owners usually have little formal training in communication, finance and strategic thinking, with a low to medium level of experience in at least a few of the remaining E Factors. The one bonus is they are used to uncertainty and have some experience of being adaptable and have both negotiation skills and marketing for business development. Some will have creativity and resilience though not many. A relatively new concept for small business owners to grasp is that they need to look after their physical and mental health and learn to use the right side of their brain to find new sustainable solutions to existing problems.

Small business owners tend not to have the time or inclination to undergo personal development either for themselves or their staff. In many cases, through a lack of long-term funding there is a challenge in making training a priority investment with related constant pressures on their time. The sector needs it, there is no doubt, but they need regional development funding to allow them to do it.

Company Executives

Company executives backed by company funding are used to attending training and development training within their industry. They all need to learn to think differently and add several of the E Factors to their existing competencies. They need to be tested on their creativity and resilience and they need to learn to promote their own projects and brand both inside and outside of the company. They need to find a new way to react to global challenges rather than using their standard company solutions. In short, they need the skills of the intrapreneur, which are remarkably like that of an entrepreneur. They need to make new things happen but still cope with corporate rules and the procedures of the company. It can be done but they need to use the E-Factor skills in a way that considers the company values and the influence of the hierarchy and senior management. There has never been a greater need for executives to use innovative and entrepreneurial E Factors to create solutions to challenges presented by technology. They need to use all the E Factors together and separately. The challenges are different, but they need innovative solutions. They must consider company culture and hierarchy, but the challenges require self-leadership creativity and resilience. Personal influencing and branding are essential. The world is changing and no matter what area we work on, constant challenges and disruption has impact on everyone and requires the skills of personal and corporate change that come from E-Factor learning.

Millennials

These are people in their thirties, at the early stage of their career who face significant challenges. It is exceedingly difficult for them to follow a set career path or to buy a house because of disruption in the world economy. Many of them have graduated from university expecting to follow the same career path and economic trajectory as their predecessors. In these disruptive times they need to take charge of their destiny and do things differently. They require better resilience to combat growing mental health problems and to take an entrepreneurial approach to their career and personal life. Otherwise they will be unable to move forward with career and personal financing steps that generations of graduates have done before them. This is quite a challenge, but they must accept the disruption and deal with the challenges and take charge of their own destiny and find their own innovative solutions.

Community Leaders

People in the community and social enterprise sectors face similar challenges to small businesses and corporates. They face reduced funding, and therefore need to create an impact to deliver many of the services that were traditionally funded by the public sector. They must create new solutions and develop effective communication strategies in order to become sustainable in the community.

There is a need to create monetary impact and get their personal brand out there. They need to negotiate deals and be resilient to find a way forward financially and achieve both economic and social impact. Management staff at all levels need the E Factor to be entrepreneurial and innovative within a social enterprise. They must demonstrate impact to their founders and find new ways to do everything.

Educators

Educators at all levels have a responsibility to educate their students to make the successful transition to their career goals and protect them from constant disruption. Secondary educators must ensure creativity and other global skills will help students to navigate life and face the constant changes and to deliver more than information. They need to influence students to act and to take charge of their own disruption. They include college lecturers and those from the universities. No matter what subject area they teach they must also develop the E-Factor competencies of the students to prepare them for the world of work and the impact of globalisation. It does not matter what their subject specialism is – they must deliver it alongside enterprise skills that will allow the students to constantly innovate, face and resolve technological challenges. They are key coaches and mentors preparing students and staff to face inevitable disruption and develop the capability to find and implement globalisation solutions.

Public Sector Managers

These roles were traditionally held by people who were suited to operating in a highly structured procedural environment and I trained many of them, one example being the entire management staff of the Child Support Agency. Like everyone else they are operating in a different environment, facing constant innovation and change. E-Factor training for public sector managers can lead to a different attitude to change and to the creation of human resources with clear development plans for global managers.

Life and Business Coaches

A coach has a key role in helping someone to achieve their objectives. A key part of their future remit will be to achieve this goal by preparing clients to face disruption and create and implement their objectives. Where possible they will often get them to think strategically and keep taking action. It is also about helping the coaches to live the E Factors and apply them in their own business and then share them with their clients who need sustainable positive change.

Students

Students of all types need to develop the skills whether in college, school or universities as they must study their subject area but also have the capacity to cope with global change. The key question is how they learn this within their existing curriculum, which – particularly in academic institutions – tends to be knowledge and subject specific content-based.

The earlier in the education cycle that the E-Factor competencies are taught the more impact will be achieved both in the educational experience but also for life in the real world after full-time education is completed.

Professionals and Academics

Professionals, for instance chartered accountants, will learn the skills and knowledge required to be a professional. They also need to learn how to face challenges and make things happen in the real world. There are many examples of people who completed their professional exams and training but do not have the business or life competencies of the E Factor to make things happen, cope with change and be a leader.

Family Businesses

Many families who work together must learn the life and business skills needed to operate successfully. Family businesses have the strength of family solidarity but generally leave it to chance as to whether the family work as a team and can innovate to find the solutions for the clients, the business and the family – a multi-generational approach is needed.

Mature Enterprise

In these changing times there is much less early retirement and many people from the age of fifty onwards are looking to find new types of work or projects. It is assumed because of their age that their life experience guarantees success. This is not necessarily so, they will find themselves operating in a new era where technology leads to new challenges and the need to be global and innovative. The E Factor is the key method to make this happen.

These are only examples of some of the core groups who need customised E-Factor training. Let's make it happen – the market is global!

Chapter 21

How Do You Change any International Organisation or Community with the E Factor?

A lot of my emphasis has been getting you to focus on separate groups of people and helping you review how you will help them understand and then help them use the E Factor in the best way to perform in changing and challenging times. I have produced strategies customised for many different target groups. It is great to have a model that anyone can use and handled right this works for everyone.

To bring a change to an organisation or a region, you will need a more comprehensive model and some back-up strategies. Sometimes you can be working with the right person or regional development lead who can easily make that transition happen. I have done it and developed a model which can guide you to make that process happen on a large or small scale.

I have managed to use the E-Factor model to change organisations, cities, ecosystems of all types and had a major impact on certain countries. It is not appropriate to name them as confidentiality means I am not allowed to do so. Certainly, my two awards from the EEC were for transforming one region and it would be unethical to release the details but what I can do is show you the model I used again to make the transformation. If you oversee a region or want advice to know how the model can have this impact, please contact me. My work email is in the book. For me it does not matter if it is changing one individual or a country – the principle is the same. Create maximum impact for others. It does not matter about the scale – the same methodology applies – though the larger the project, the more factors that need to be considered.

So, what is the name of the model? It's called the ELVIS model. What am I saying? That you need to sing songs like Elvis the famous pop star to change people, regions or countries? That's an idea and he was a great performer and a great singer! In my lifelong quest to use the E Factor to change people, organisations, regions and countries I like to describe some Elvis lyrics that encapsulate my mixed feelings with trying to create worldwide impact and change: 'Caught in a trap, I can't let go because I love you too much baby'. Isn't that how we feel sometimes about our work, our relationships, our life!

The letters ELVIS highlight the key areas you must use to change organisations, regions and countries.

E is for E Factor.

L is for linking up the entrepreneurial ecosystem.

V is for verification of outcomes – you must prove that change has happened and measure the impact.

I is for institutional support where the senior management must strongly support the initiative and build it into their strategy and funding package to have maximum effect.

S is for stakeholder support, which is needed on a major scale for change to happen – for a university this would be senior management, staff students, regional government, major funders, and major external customers, to name a few.

To show how it works I will take you through how I applied it to use the E Factor to change a university on a vast and sustainable scale. I started off by sharing the E-Factor model with department heads, the students' union and the regional development unit. I then shared it with all key stakeholders, including government representatives in Northern Ireland. I put the E Factor into the core curriculum of all fifty subject areas at the university. Even the thought of it exhausts me now.

What I did next was powerful. I linked everyone into a committee, and we met monthly with the leaders of all key units involved. I also linked curriculum and extra-curricular activities and created a seamless system for staff and students. To be fair, the pro-vice chancellor had an excellent committee that had met for three years and when I made some impact, they supported me to the hilt.

I then used verification by measuring changes in students and staff, both through recording business starts and other successes, carrying out longitudinal research with over 15,000 students measuring their E-Factor competency scores to highlight the effectiveness of the model, and published ten academic journals on it.

I worked constantly on institutional support both on a practical level through strong written communication and working closely with senior management.

I also worked with a range of internal and external supporters to keep them informed and got huge support. An incredible model, but it could not have worked without stakeholders and senior management communicating at the highest level on their support and making my model their main project to highlight regionally nationally and internationally. Trips to major international leaders followed and many key awards that enhanced the university's reputation in entrepreneurship education worldwide. The ELVIS model and the E Factor won the Times Higher Entrepreneurial University of the year award. I personally won the Times Higher Most Innovative Educator in the UK for ELVIS and the best postgraduate researcher award.

The Higher Education Academy – the key university education body – also gave me an award for being the most innovative educator in the UK. This again ensured senior management and stakeholder support and led to further global impact advising the Indian government and training fifty senior executives from the EEC for two weeks at Queens. I did over eighty keynotes regionally and globally over five years. The accolades included the only OBE ever awarded for enterprise education and numerous overseas visiting professorships.

You can see how the model applied and after leaving Queens in 2013 I created a new ELVIS model for the Liverpool region between 2015 and 2017. I was head of Entrepreneurship Education with a lot of day-to-day duties with students on a one-to-one basis and with no direct access to senior management. If I was going to have impact, I was going to have to change my model to fit in with the new circumstances and lack of resources.

Quite a challenge. Could ELVIS work one more time? I was up for the challenge. I knew it would be tricky without senior management support and so I knew I had to apply the model in a unique way. Like all good E-Factor practitioners I would have to be creative, resilient and strategic and, of course, use my ELVIS model to analyse how to get the E Factor to the region of Liverpool, as well as Liverpool John Moores University.

I took the opportunity to teach the E Factor to student classes I was assigned to and got student advocates who endorsed what I did. I realised there was no way I could embed it, teach in every discipline, and spend time on promoting and designing new materials as well as taking it internationally. I did take the model to some senior managers with a mixed response. I needed to produce a solution that could reach as many staff, students and stakeholders as early as possible. Finally, after my six o'clock in the morning creativity and brainstorming practice I was rewarded with a Eureka moment and the answer. That provided satisfactory proof that creativity practice is where you start, so the answer was clear: create a community of practice of educators at Liverpool John Moores and from local colleges. Not as easy as you imagine. The first meeting was a failure – or a learning experience as I like to call it. Only two out of a thousand educators showed up and I never saw or heard from it again. What a wonderful opportunity to walk my talk and find Plan B instead of thinking it was all over.

I developed an innovative marketing strategy. I invited an Australian contact of mine in Enterprise Education who was a great keynote speaker and very international – Colin, who travelled extensively with a great budget, which was good because unlike Queens I didn't have one at Liverpool John Moores University! I marketed the seminar with no budget but used social media emails and every contact I had at the university. I had three weeks to build it and there were over one hundred educators in the room. It was a remarkable success and I built on that and maintained the community of practice, mentoring the group on an ongoing basis with at least one monthly meeting, and every day I met or mentored at least five of the group. It was an unbelievable success.

I linked it to the Liverpool Ecosystem and built strong links with a very inspirational mayor who brought the Liverpool council and many people of influence to support the education community. The impact was amazing, and we measured it – over 400 educators from Liverpool John Moores and many from other local institutions, reaching a student population of over 30,000!

They all taught the E Factor with my materials and the project led to E-Factor success in USA, China, Europe and Cambridge University. Next thing I knew, I had a senior Chinese academic from the UK government sitting next to me learning the E Factor! I Googled him, and he is now the top professor in his university! He has the E Factor.

ELVIS was followed to the letter. It was linked to the Liverpool Ecosystem, verified significant student and staff behavioural change but also measured increased startups and impactful staff development. Senior management then backed it, and it had stakeholders right through Liverpool. The university, unlike Queens, had never won any national awards. Within two years it won best UK programme, best programme in Europe, the Times Higher Education Award and the ultimate – the USASBE (the United States Association for Small Business and Entrepreneurship) Best Global Program award. Which means the best in the world.

It had been easier and was nothing like the experience I had at Queens. I had the model to make it happen and the E Factor worked.

The key lesson is that you can achieve whatever you want if you use the E Factor and help others to do the same. Follow ELVIS and you know what you have to do, not only to create it but sustain it. I do honestly believe whoever you are and whatever your aims you can achieve them with the E-Factor model. Feel free to ask for advice if you need any, be it a small or large project!

My examples are clearly based on a university model, quite challenging institutions to change due to their highly bureaucratic structure and multiple stakeholders. You will find it much easier in other types of communities or institutions. The important lesson, as well as applying the model, is to take time to understand it, its aims, objectives, strengths, and weaknesses. Then customise the model. If I could do these things with zero budgets and little help, I believe you could do much more. It's learning the model, applying it and being clear what you want to achieve. Always start at the beginning and sort yourself out first before helping others. There is plenty of help there and feel free to contact me as a reader of this new book. Let me know what you need, and I will at least give you some suggestions to work on. Hopefully, you are now part of the global E Factor community of practice!

Chapter 22

E-Factor Case Studies

A lot of my examples up to now have been showing you how the E Factor has had an impact on large universities. This is partly because that is where I created the E Factor and where I used the model to create massive organisational change and impact. The model has been taught to a wide range of stakeholders and if you contact me, I can give you multiple examples of various types of user, different organisations, and people with different objectives to the ones I had, which was to change students, staff and management in universities. It can be used anywhere, and I propose to give you several different case studies that show the different purposes that people are using the E Factor for throughout the world. With some of the cases I will talk about the actual person involved and in some cases I will not give their name to allow them privacy. It is important that you understand that the E Factor can be used in any industry, any country, and any situation. There are times I wish I had come up with a model that was for a much smaller niche – maybe all fifty-year-old executives in a small town in my local area! The global application possibilities both in industry and region creates huge opportunities, but huge challenges. I love it but as I become more mature, I need to think about handing it over to the next generation. I could give you thousands of live case studies and hundreds of potential markets but there is just time and space in this book for a few focused examples. The best answer may be to create a global community of practice where we will support each other and share our ideas and learnings. Here's five small case studies to start.

1. Brennan Williams is a Welshman living and working in South Africa. He uses the E-Factor model to diagnose entrepreneurial weaknesses and weaknesses of startup entrepreneurs in a rural setting. He has helped thousands of startups and created many sustainable businesses because he has identified their E-Factor strengths and weaknesses with the model and helped them to address the weaknesses and work on their strengths. His reach within South Africa is growing all the time.

2. Craig Dickson (name changed) has used the E Factor to help hundreds of graduate apprentices in the UK to create new projects and develop as industry executives. They take the questionnaire regularly and have created social enterprises using the E Factor to function as an innovative team.

3. John Willis (name changed) has used the E Factor to help with management development in the north of England. The participants used the model to analyse their organisation, to develop leadership skills and to create strategic

collaborations in a public sector environment whilst still measuring global impact.

4. Rita Mallon (name changed) is a well-being practitioner. She helps people build resilience and has added the other seven E Factors to their portfolio to ensure they become more proactive and turn their challenges into business opportunities.

5. William Daniels (name changed) is using the E Factor as a model to allow companies and executives to change their personal and business lives and have a greater impact on the community.

It's a rough tough old world at times. You have just read the E Factor, and you understand that the competency can help you to be more objective and achieve your goals. Sounds great! What's the problem? Game over? Sadly, no, it's only the start! Just because you know a skill is important and how to use it does not mean you have it, can use it unconsciously and create the results you need. You need to make it a daily habit, something you use and apply without thinking – just as you have three coffees a day. Some people are good at acquiring new habits and applying them straight away but most of us struggle unless it's something we do or use without thinking. I have given various tips throughout the book, but I have come back to take a final focus on what you can do daily and as your coach enable you to achieve impact in whatever you are doing by using the E Factors automatically in the right situation to achieve the best results.

I do understand it's not an easy process to change bad or ineffectual habits but a very necessary one. Without the right habits any project you work on will be undermined as it's the right daily impact that creates sustainable results. You may need to change long-standing habits and create new ones and the behaviour around all eight factors must become a habit or you will seriously undermine your personal and corporate effectiveness. Perhaps every so often you will be able to make things happen. However, in the 21st century it's what you do every day that counts as you face constant new challenges and disruption because of technology and globalisation.

We need to use positive and negative reinforcement as part of the process. You first need to see the benefits that the E Factor can bring you. For instance, looking at creativity – are you finding new solutions to ongoing problems and coming up with ideas that can do everything from boosting efficiency to making a huge breakthrough of your choice? Can you see the benefit of the new competency for yourself? Can you see what it could do for others? Then you need to take the steps to implement. Also, how you begin your day is very important and will increase the chances of it becoming a habit. Can you give yourself a reward for the first three times you use it? Who is keeping you accountable? Find someone who will ask you the hard questions. No matter what, your amygdala will create initial anxiety, but work on your relaxation. If you can get to two months, keep a journal, have rewards set up for completion and get the support. I managed to develop the habit four years ago of running 5 km each morning at 6 am. By doing this, it sets me up for the day with a clear mind. I have never missed a day, even when away from home. If I can do it, you can do it. What E Factor are you going to start with? Use relaxation and mindfulness to keep you calm and keep your emotions in check.

Developing a growth mindset will really help and keep asking yourself questions that will inspire you. How will this habit help me? How will it help me to inspire others? Very simply, if we can learn to focus on one change at a time and decrease multitasking this will make you more productive.

Get good at making decisions and choices. Learn from everyone, both from the good projects and the ones that went disastrously wrong. Design the decision-making process that works best for you and your team.

Be clear what the habits are that you want to change and which ones you want to maintain. Make sure they will enhance your use of the E Factor. The key thing is to practise every day. No matter what you do, it's important to get constant honest feedback on a regular basis and remain humble and open to learning. Most of all what you need are daily routines where you use and practise the good habits and they become an integral part of your daily activity. Starting your day with creativity and resilience is good. Focus during the day on using your communication skills for personal branding, personal influence and negotiation. Keep using your imagination, like you did as a child – imagination builds your creativity skills immensely. Use the end of the day to reflect on personal and financial results and set a short plan for the next day. You can do this, I know. Build the habits and the competencies stage by stage. Use them in non-serious interventions, learn and refine them. You can have anything you want by just learning and developing the right habits one step at a time.

Go for it!

Conclusion

Yes, we have reached the end of this book, but of course I feel it is only the beginning. I have given as much information and guidance as I can, and I hope you will have found it interesting and extremely helpful. The model works, it is now up to you to do what you want with it.

Thank you for your time and there is one thing I am sure of: you can do this, and I wish both great learnings and great success on your journey. I hope I have made you aware about the threats and opportunities we face in the global economy. You have the capability to survive all the challenges and to take all the opportunities that the Fourth Industrial Revolution brings. Be curious and keep adapting and you will be well prepared for the future, and the impact of new technology.

There are opportunities everywhere so keep looking around for them, keep asking for them. Decide what you want and take the steps you need to achieve this. It is important to be a lifelong learner and to use the E Factors to create results.

Build new networks and learn new things as often as you can. Technology will bring you opportunities to learn, innovate and create. Of all the E Factors to embrace the most vital is creativity, followed by resilience, as things change rapidly in a globally and interconnected world. Develop your skills and competencies and welcome the disruption and opportunities that come your way. You will be one of the winners from globalisation and technological change, I am sure of it.

Take good care of yourself, your colleagues and your community. We all perform better and are stronger when we are connected.

The world is yours and full of opportunities we have never seen before. Enjoy, go for it, and help others along the way.

You are the future, and the world is yours!

Professor David Gibson, OBE

Execute the Plan

This is a chapter I have added in to help you implement the E Factor.

I want to make sure you apply the E Factor and achieve the success you deserve. The original book was well received, won many awards and I learnt some key lessons that I want to share with you to improve your effectiveness.

The original E Factor was endorsed by many people, including the president of the United States of America. Many people read the book but didn't know how to create the habits so they could use the E Factor to achieve their ambitions. All eight of the E Factors are practical skills/habits which will enable anyone to achieve success, provided the skills have become automatic and can be applied in a practical situation.

Each E Factor can be used individually or together to create results. Read the book and make the competencies part of your skill set and then individually or as a team make the project or change happen. It will take a little time and effort to practise the skills, but it's well worth it. Understand the skills. How and when will you apply them to achieve personal and organisational objectives? Use them and make them part of your skill set and achieve the success you crave and deserve.

A few things that will make an immediate difference. First, practise and use your E-Factor model until you are confident to use it in any situation. Use some of the competencies at least once a month in a real-life situation. Keep reading the materials and think about future situations where you could use them.

Monthly use the questionnaire and see how your skills are improving and work on any potential weaknesses. What goals do you want to achieve and who do you want to help? You are aiming for unconscious competence and the only way is to practise and use all the E Factors, as often as you can.

You are searching for profound knowledge that you can apply in a practical situation. You are also setting an example for other people who have been introduced to the model and, like you, need to develop the real-life competence.

Keep a record and hold yourself accountable. Even better, find someone to report to. This can make such a difference. Eventually, if you persevere you will begin to use the skills automatically. You will be more effective and inspire others to do the same.

There is nothing more frustrating than having knowledge and access to skills and not using them as part of your work strategy. There are many who do this. It's like having a million pounds in a safe that you never use to help yourself or others.

Cultivate a growth mindset as advocated by Dr Carol Dweck, a leading American psychologist who wrote the book *Mindset: The New Psychology of Success*. Work on areas you can control. Enjoy learning and persevere until using the E Factor is something you do every day. Your behaviour and use of the competency will become automatic. It may not be possible to use all eight every single day but do not lose sight of your objective.

Your objective is to use the E Factors separately and together daily, so that they are part of your behaviour automatically. If you can achieve this then, as they say, the world really will be your oyster!

Form your own community of practice with other people who are also trying to integrate it into their life. Be refreshingly honest with each other but supportive. Every day is a learning day with the E Factor.

The good thing is that the E Factor can help people in a range of situations and is already proven internationally. Every situation you face can be improved by using one or more of the E Factors.

Let me give you a couple of examples where it has helped individuals and organisations and how my E Factor graduate used the model to help entrepreneurs, executives, students and educators.

Brennan Williams is a mentor to small businesses in South Africa, and he is having tremendous results using the E Factor with over three thousand small businesses. This is a notable example of how the E Factor is being used.

Using and practising the E-Factor competencies has enabled a range of people with limited funding to create a business, be resilient and keep learning. Most importantly they have found funding, built their personal brand, and got sales. This highlights the power of the model.

In Carlisle, England, over one hundred educators were certified to use the E Factor with their college classes. The educators developed the skills to enhance their career and ensure the college had greater impact with business clients' students and helped and supported entrepreneurs throughout Cumbria.

Within the nuclear industry over one hundred graduate apprentices were trained in the E Factor and used the competency model to develop eight highly successful social enterprises, enabling them to have regional and global impact.

These are just some of the success stories and we are determined to add more with the help of this new book.

You will find your own way to keep using the E Factor and help others to do the same. Being competent and using all eight competencies in group and individual situations can enhance your contribution and your own personal and business goals.

I hope you have enjoyed the book and will learn from these true examples. Work on your own development and help others to learn and develop the skills of the 21st century!

Knowledge must be used first for yourself, and then to assist others. The E Factor can help you do this if you make it part of your life. Go for it!

About the Author

Professor David Gibson, OBE is an internationally recognised expert on Entrepreneurship Education. He has taught and guided many people to develop entrepreneurial competencies to enhance their career, become successful and helped others. He created and developed the E-Factor model which incorporates all eight E-Factor skills to become more entrepreneurial. He has won forty-five national and international awards for the impact of his work. The late Queen awarded him the OBE in 2012 for his contribution to education.

Professor Gibson lives in a small coastal village in Ireland and is currently Head of Entrepreneurship Education at Cumbria University.

You can contact Professor Gibson at: davidalexgibson@ icloud.com

Index

morning routine, 129
purpose, 129
share your story, 130
see also creativity;
   finance; leadership;
   negotiation; personal
   branding; personal
   influence; resilience;
   strategic thinking
E-Factor skill model,
   original, 110, 112
Einstein, Albert, 131
Elizabeth II, Queen, 104
ELVIS model, 162–7
equity investors, 29
ethics, 76
exercise, 100
exit plan, 99, 146

F
failure, 146
family businesses, 159
feedback, 5, 173
finance, 17–32
   employee, 30–1
   funding, 28–30, 107
   negotiation skills, 26
   profile on and offline, 26
   public sector, 29, 30, 31
   rules of money
      management, 19–20
   sources of, 20
   success, 21–2

technology and, 23–4, 31
financial competence, 19
financial grants, 20
financial habits, 20, 24–7
financial jargon, 19,
   20, 22–3, 28
financial plan, 31–2
financial qualifications, 27–8
five C's (clarity, consistency,
   content, confidence and
   commitment), 55
flexibility, 127
food, healthy, 6
Fourth Industrial
   Revolution, 3, 33, 40,
   60, 71, 109, 112, 115,
   120, 142, 150, 151, 175

G
Generation Z, 151
global community of
   practice, 152, 170
growth mindset, 178

H
history of the E Factor
   2005–2024, 139–43
honesty, 5, 76, 77, 107
humility, 99, 100,
   106, 134, 173

I
integrity, 76
intention, setting, 117